Equity Detectives:
ADVANCING EEO
INVESTIGATION
Methods

Equity Detectives: ADVANCING EEO INVESTIGATION Methods

EEO Investigations Decoded:
A Practical Approach

ADVANCED EEO SOLUTIONS

Advanced EEO Solutions
Company email: info@advancedeeosolutions.com
Company website: https://advancedeeosolutions.com/

Equity Detectives: Advancing EEO Investigation Methods, Advanced EEO Solutions—1st ed.

DEDICATION

In life you have people that influence you with their love and guidance, through their stories and gentle lessons. When you are young you do not understand or appreciate those lessons until later in life. Our Grandmothers were those people. The stories, the hardships, and the efforts they took to explain complex concepts so a child could comprehend. Their efforts have not been forgotten, as they are beneficial to us in adulthood. A dedication to all the Grandparents that have positively shaped the future for all of us.

Susie Hamilton Washington: (1926 – 2001)

Her grandparents were former slaves in the deep south of Mississippi. She was born in 1921 under Jim Crow laws and a few years later lived through the Great Depression as a child. She graduated high school early, applied for positions up north, and movement to D.C. as a teenager prior to the Civil and Women's Rights movement. She worked for the federal government while obtaining undergraduate and graduate degrees. She decided on a career in education and retired as a High School grade Principal. In retirement, she volunteered to prepare taxes for those in need and spent time traveling to visit her family. In her short life, she had experienced uncertainty, persevered, obtained success, and gave back. She made an extra effort to continuously plant seeds of knowledge during her grandson's adolescence so that he understood the pillars of success later in his life. He learned a valuable lesson; Make continuous efforts to educate, improve, and sustain yourself, but make sure to help others with what you have obtained.

Lidia Haetskaya: (1935- 2007)

Grandma Lidia was born in 1935 on a small family farm. While her younger brother received an education she was never sent to school because it was considered unnecessary for a woman to know how to read and write. At a country ball, at the age of 16, she met her husband. Her husband was offered a job in a big newly developed city, and they moved there to start a family. Lidia's husband loved reading and they spent their evenings teaching her to read and write. Unfortunately, by the age of 29, she was left a widower, a stranger in a town with two young girls. She worked as a helper to the cook at the local diner. Subsequently, she became the head cook and became popular for her cooking skills. People from neighboring cities and villages, from various social classes came to eat at her diner. She never turned away a person that was hungry or in need. When people addressed her, they called her "Mother Lidia" because that is what she was to everyone. She would treat them as if they were her kids, with love. Because she never received an education, she made sure that both of her girls went to college sacrificing everything. She had to alter her own dresses to fit her girls leaving her with only 2 dresses for herself. When the soles of her shoe were worn out, she would cut cardboard and put it inside. She worked long hours until late at night, came home, and baked so she could sell those baked goods.

She would always tell us "Always share your bread and ask your guest to join you for tea. You never know the person's journey so don't assume that it was an easy one."

CONTENTS

INDUSTRY EXPERIENCE

Advanced EEO Solutions (AES) has hands-on experience in Title VII Equal Employment Opportunity (EEO) Investigations with over 30 federal government agencies, facilitating more than 3,500 EEO complaints as of 2023.

Facts about AES's experience with EEO Investigations

1. AES is a Prime Contractor that manages EEO service contracts for the federal government.
2. AES's co-founder and Principal is a certified EEO Investigator and has experience investigating hundreds of complaints, performing sufficiency reviews of thousands of cases, and facilitating over 3,500 cases.
3. AES's Principal used to conduct the required 32-hour training course for New Investigator certification.
4. AES mentors and provides technical instruction on how to conduct sufficient EEO Investigations.
5. AES has experience managing hundreds of independent EEO Investigators.
6. AES was the SBA 2020 Subcontractor of the Year for providing Program Management services on an EEO Service contract.

7. AES specializes in customized training to educate EEO Investigators on areas of concern.
8. AES focuses on training Investigators, rather than making corrections.
9. AES directly communicates and works with EEO Specialists, Managers, and Directors that relay specifically what they expect in a Report of Investigation.
10. AES has worked on two of the largest EEO service contracts in the federal government.

AES facilitates EEO Investigations daily as part of its business model. Our experience and guidance will provide valuable insight for professionals in the industry.

INTRODUCTION

This book is a practical guide for conducting EEO Investigations and producing effective Reports of Investigation (ROI).

Conducting EEO Investigations can be a rewarding career where an Investigator's effort can make a difference in mitigating alleged employment discrimination. EEO Investigators can impact people's lives because employment law applies to every U.S. employee of working age. People are diverse in race, color, age, sex, gender or sexual orientation, national origin, religion, disability, genetic condition, and if they have participated in protected activity. Employment discrimination is a pertinent topic for discussion, discovery, instruction, and implementation.

The origins of employment law can be traced back to the Industrial Revolution. However, many employees do not know their employment rights, have never met an EEO Investigator, and are not aware that Investigations are conducted into discrimination complaints in the workplace.

Let's start with the basics.

Certified EEO Investigators are neutral fact finders for complaints of discrimination. Although EEO Investigators are qualified to handle management inquiries, while others are skilled to facilitate workplace investigations and private sector discrimination complaints, this book will focus on aspects specific to federal EEO complaints under Title VII.

Certified EEO Investigators take an initial 32 hours of required training on Employment Law theories and statutes, and eight hours each year going forward. EEO Investigators are independent consultants that should be qualified to produce a sufficient investigation and ROI.

Industry concern

Advanced EEO Solutions (AES) has found that only 3 of 10 Investigators are proficient in investigating and submitting a sufficient ROI without assistance. AES has worked with hundreds of Investigators over the last 15 years and AES's founder has deemed it necessary to customize a quality control system due to the amount of poor-quality draft ROIs regularly submitted. The work product was not sufficient to submit to our federal government clients. Not only new Investigators, but Investigators with varying years of experience have struggled to produce a quality work product. Inadequate training and a lack of specific skills which will be discussed in this book, is the reason many Investigators perform poorly.

Solution

This is **not** one of those books that excites you with fluff, presents a problem, and then provides a solution which is a sales pitch for an expensive training that the author happens to offer. This **is** the book that will provide EEO professionals with both practical instructions on how to produce effective EEO Investigations and valuable insight into the skills required to succeed. Investigators must invest in themselves if they desire to be successful.

Who will benefit?

Now that you have obtained a copy of this book, if you invest time in skills training by following our instructions, we guarantee that you will elevate your career as an EEO Investigator or acquire invaluable insight on EEO investigations that will help your career in a related industry. Our instruction is not only for the novice; seasoned practitioners have also benefited from our method of conducting EEO Investigations. This book is not meant to imitate a 32-hour training requirement but is rather a "beyond the 32 hours" instructional guide to delivering a high-quality product.

Our instructions are beneficial to many different people and professions: EEO Investigators and Counselors, EEO Specialists/Managers/Directors/DEIA, etc., Employment Law Attorneys, Private Sector HR Professionals, Employment Law School students, Complainants filing a discrimination complaint, and Investigators in other industries.

Understanding some specific skills required, and implementing some key techniques provided in this book will improve EEO Investigations and generate quality Reports of Investigation. Qualified EEO professionals have noteworthy careers, as they can directly impact and play a part in addressing workplace discrimination.

CHAPTER 1

The Problem

As many say in the Agency, "There is no perfect investigation." This is a statement coined by Agency Officials that deal with EEO complaints. In fact, the Stakeholders in the industry have addressed issues with the quality of work provided by many EEO Contractors and their Subcontractors (the EEO Investigators) dating back to early 2000, when the Government Accountability Office (GOA) addressed concerns with EEO processes. Below, see the following public information and data detailing feedback from stakeholders.

Data/GAO report: Not only do unnecessary and time-consuming processes hinder the prompt investigation of federal sector complaints, but they may also result in additional costs to the government in salaries and other costs associated with the investigation. For example, at one agency we found that the time spent by agency staff in repeated reviews of the same contractor investigative plan, in some cases, still resulted in agency staff having to supplement the investigation after the contractor's final investigative report was provided to the agency. Therefore, additional costs are incurred by these repeated reviews of investigative plans and in supplementing the contractor's final work product. Not only may delays in investigating complaints impede the primary goal of gathering sufficient evidence to permit a determination as to whether discrimination occurred, but it may also affect the livelihood and well-being of individuals who believe they have been discriminated against.

GAO report: In its 2004 report on federal sector EEO investigations and cost, EEOC cited the importance of federal agencies *having EEO programs staffed with employees who have the necessary knowledge, skills, and abilities to help reduce the time it takes to conduct investigations. More than three-quarters of the survey respondents from the agencies and EEOC as well as plaintiffs' attorneys pointed to the importance of investigators enhancing their current level of knowledge and skills in the federal EEO complaint process.*

Data: *Remands: Of the 1,548 dismissal appeals EEOC received in fiscal 2012, nearly 700 were remanded back to the agency. Remands lead to having to divide the allocated money from the budget to Re-Investigate the same complaint. Putting a strain on the Agency budget, postponing the process way beyond 180.*

It is a critical concern that these problems date back almost 20 years and continue to this day. There are multiple reasons why some Investigators are not effective, or why ROIs are not considered high quality. AES will address **three (3) main reasons** for some of the mediocre quality identified in EEO Investigations.

---

3 Reasons for Poor Quality EEO Investigations:
- **Limited Practical Training**
- **Not having the proper resources**
- **Lack of Commitment**

Reason number one is **a lack of practical and thorough training.**

Practical Training: In the introduction, it was mentioned that 32 hours of training is required to be a certified EEO Investigator. However, much of that training is theory-based, and very few Investigators can effectively facilitate an EEO Investigation after the training course.

AES has experienced many Investigators coming fresh out of training who are not able to draft effective questions, are not familiar with general templates, have limited knowledge of general protocols used during the investigative stage in federal cases, and have little to no experience interviewing, asking follow-up questions, identifying key witnesses, assembling cases, or summarizing the Affidavits. Many of these new Investigators still need training and lack pertinent skills to make them an effective Investigator. Since much of their training is based on theory and case law curriculum, they are not privy to what is expected of them in terms of drafting an ROI. Being able to regurgitate case law, theories, and industry terms are not the skills necessary to effectively investigate an EEO complaint.

Newly certified Investigators will learn many of the vital skills through hands-on application after they have been assigned their first case; however, the Agency expects quality regardless of an Investigator's experience.

Another part of the problem is that some experienced Investigators have displayed a lack of skills or bad habits from dated protocols, which require obtaining updated training on practices, using current templates, and changing their investigative strategies.

Investigators are required to take eight hours of additional training each year to remain certified. The refresher courses are not customized to assess an individual's performance issues; these refreshers usually go over new case law and best practices.

An Investigator needs a trainer or mentor who will take the time to review their work, identify errors and suggest corrections, provide feedback, and utilize custom real-life scenarios as teaching opportunities to focus on specific area(s) where the Investigator most needs to improve. An advanced training curriculum will show Investigators how to apply theoretical knowledge, answer tough questions, and will specifically demonstrate how to provide a comprehensive ROI. AES will provide that instruction throughout this book.

Reason number two **is the lack of proper resources which causes the Investigator to appear unprofessional and amateurish.**

Having the necessary equipment, ample time, and a professional work environment allows the Investigator to be organized and efficient. Investigators work remotely, which was the standard even before the COVID-19 pandemic.

Below are some examples that illustrate unprofessionalism in an EEO Investigator.

(1) While the Investigator is on telephonic interviews, there is background noise (crying babies, television/radio, barking dogs).

(2) The Investigator uses a cell phone with bad reception to conduct an interview.

(3) The Investigator does not have a scanner, has an outdated computer that "crashes" once a month, or uses an

inappropriate email address for EEO investigations, e.g. "LoveJazz@gmail.com"

(4) The Investigator accepts an assignment with a specific deadline, but halfway through the investigation, informs the case manager that they have a vacation planned at the same time the case is due.

(5) The Investigator's voice mailbox is often full, or their internet/email is frequently out of service.

(6) The Investigator accidentally commingles case information due to a lack of organization and a proper filing system.

(7) The Investigator has other engagements and is not available during business hours to manage their cases or to conduct timely interviews.

(8) The Investigator does not use external hard drives to back up their information in case of power outages or computer crashes.

(9) The technology they use is outdated and they are unable to utilize recommended systems to produce ROIs or to upload their work using file-sharing sites, e.g., Adobe Acrobat Pro DC and OneDrive.

In the typical work world, these issues are resolved by the employer providing the necessary office space, equipment, up-to-date technology, and filing systems. Oftentimes, a typical employee will have access to resources such as an IT help desk and training programs. As mentioned, since EEO Investigators work remotely the onus is on them to operate like an efficient and successful business.

Reason number three is **Lack of Commitment.**

The cliché statement "this is not for everyone" is often used in the industry because this is definitely a field that is not suited for everyone. There is a steep learning curve in training to conduct EEO Investigations. Effective EEO Investigators are dedicated to continuous learning through constant development of new skills and are able to accept constructive criticism.

AES believes the Investigator's motivating purpose for deciding to do EEO investigations directly impacts the commitment required to be effective. Some people enter the industry for the wrong reasons, e.g., the desire to work remotely, to avoid corporate politics, or only to supplement their income without having any interest in employment discrimination. Having a sense of purpose or, better yet, a real passion for the work will reduce the learning curve and incentivize professionals for the continuous growth it takes to produce quality EEO Investigations.

Below are some examples that illustrate the wrong intention or show a lack of purpose or commitment to doing EEO Investigations.

1. **Investigators have abandoned their cases when matters get complicated.**

   Key Point: There are easier ways to make money than doing EEO Investigations. Some will provide mediocre quality or just "cut losses" and disappear.

2. **There are a select few Investigators who take on too many cases in order to meet a financial goal, to the point where the workload is unmanageable, and it is impossible to provide quality investigations.**

Key Point: "You must crawl before you can walk." Some rush into a large caseload without experience in strategic planning or putting in the effort to hone their organizational skills.

3. **Some Investigators have a poor work ethic and refuse to take responsibility for errors, lateness, and inappropriate actions.**

   Key Point: EEO Investigations require the development of various skills and diverse case experience, both of which naturally take time and patience in order to reduce errors and provide both a timely and quality ROI.

4. **ROIs are sloppy, testimony is missing, documents are out of order, there are gaps in testimony, and issues may not be covered thoroughly.**

   Key Point: As stated in Number 3, Investigators need to commit ample time to acquiring new skills, taking additional training, and working on areas with which they struggle.

5. **Experienced Investigators can be reluctant to update their skills and implement new protocols, and when asked to make changes, they respond, "I have been doing it like this for 15 years."**

   Key Point: Laws are constantly updated, protocols are adjusted, new directives are mandated, and technology is introduced that increases efficiency. Some Investigators use outdated and ineffective practices, and the quality of their investigations inevitably suffers.

6. **As a result of Number 5, Investigators who refuse to accept new practices, technology, and changes in the field are often difficult to work with and create unnecessary extra effort for the other people involved in the complaints process.**

   Key Point: There must be a committed and continuous effort to improve EEO Investigations.

Most EEO professionals have lives outside of their careers, but the Investigators who are not successful are usually unable or unwilling to commit the time and effort necessary to thoroughly investigate their cases. They are out of the office frequently, take extended vacations too often, and do not designate enough time in their schedules to hone their skills, implement best practices, and obtain further knowledge through research and training. These select individuals without a good sense of purpose lack the dedication it takes to produce quality EEO Investigations on a continuous basis.

The next chapter will address current performance concerns and explain in technical detail the signs of poor training, work ethic, and EEO knowledge that need to be addressed to improve the quality of EEO Investigations.

CHAPTER 2

Stakeholder Survey

This chapter will discuss the common pet peeves for EEO professionals that review and utilize ROIs. We will address specific concerns with EEO Investigators' work products, EEO Investigations in general, and the final ROIs. We will address the concerns relayed by stakeholders in chronological fashion, based on the order of the complaints process: Vendor's review, Agency's review, FAD Writer's Review, and lastly the Administrative Judge's review.

Our goal is to inform and educate our readers to ignite that spark in the individual to criticize their own work so that they can make the necessary adjustments to improve and increase the quality of their EEO Investigations. Effective change(s) can only be made when problems are specifically identified and assessed, and practical solutions are implemented.

The information AES is providing in this chapter was obtained through industry research and feedback. This information will significantly reduce the time it takes to address common concerns and implement solutions within the EEO complaints process. It is more efficient to learn from another Investigator's errors so that compliance and quality can be achieved quicker, or common mishaps can be avoided. Investigators work independently on cases; therefore, they are not privy to all the best practices or major concerns relayed by stakeholders as well as all the best practices, tips, and tricks used by other Investigators. Surprisingly, the same errors have continued over a span of 20 years, and this book is the first step in providing a continuing solution.

Vendor Review:

As a Vendor, AES performs hundreds of sufficiency reviews on ROIs each year. It is typical for multiple problems to occur during the investigative stage. To overcome these roadblocks, Investigators need specific resources, skills, practical experience, mentors, and an understanding of current directives. We have identified the following common shortcomings or mistakes that Investigators encounter during the investigative process, which can be fixed with the proper instruction.

1. **Inability to follow specific directions.**
   Ex: When a template is provided, Investigators change the formatting, and font size, or enter data in the wrong sections making the ROI inconsistent, which appears unprofessional.

2. **Failure to immediately review the affidavits and ask follow-up questions during the investigative stage.**
   Ex: The RMO stated he made the decision based on a directive from his first-line Supervisor, but the Investigator failed to ask what the directive specified, and the reasons for that directive, and did not ask for the name of the first-line Supervisor.

3. **Not interviewing all relevant witnesses under reasonable circumstances.**

   Ex: The Investigator interviews two of the four panel members that made the recommendation to refer the applicant (Complainant) to the Selecting Official.

4. **Lack of attention to detail - not proofreading ROIs, emails, correspondence, or affidavits.**

   Ex: The Investigator addresses recipients by the wrong name, gender identity, or rank/position, or misspells names. This could easily make someone question the validity of the investigation.

5. **Copying/pasting everything from affidavits and not summarizing testimony in chronological order.**

   Ex: The ROI Summary switches points of view, i.e., some parts of the summary are written in first person and the others in third person.

6. **Summarizing irrelevant testimony, using too many quotations without summarizing, or failing to summarize background information to relay the context.**

   Ex: "The RMO is my supervisor, he let the discrimination occur and I heard he did it at his previous job." This direct quote lacks pertinent details and clarity and is hearsay evidence.

7. **The Request for Documents is too broad or vague which may result in voluminous documents that are irrelevant or redundant.**

   Ex: The Investigator makes a request for the Agency to provide data on all employees who received deficient performance appraisals for a period of two years, annotated by race. This request needs to be narrowed down to extract only the employees in a comparable situation.

8. **Using only generic, open-ended, or incomplete questions.**
   Ex: "How did you feel about it?" "Tell me what occurred when you were terminated?" "Is national origin the reason for discrimination?" The specific wording of questions will affect the quality of response received.

9. **Losing control of the investigation.**
   Ex: The Complainant influences the Investigator to interview witnesses from a prior complaint to prove a point in their current complaint. Investigators need to determine the appropriate purview and not be swayed off track.

10. **Not using a Memorandum to the File (MTF) to address information missing from the file, or not documenting the MTF with supporting evidence.**
    Ex: The Complainant's witnesses were not interviewed because they were unresponsive to the Investigator's attempts to contact them. There is no MTF with supporting documentation to explain or prove this; it appears that the Investigator did not make an attempt and the investigation will be considered incomplete.

11. **Using the wrong Complainant name, agency, case number, or protected class(es) on a consistent basis.**
    Ex: Investigators have consistently referred to the wrong protected classes throughout the ROI summary or

used information relevant to other cases. This could be considered a PII violation, if not effectively addressed.

12. **Interviewing all suggested witnesses without determining who is relevant.**
    Ex: Interviewing the Complainant's mom as a character witness, or witnesses that can only offer hearsay. Testimony should be unbiased and exhibit evidence that is direct, circumstantial, or comparative.

13. **Not following the chain of command.**
    Ex: The Investigator copies the EEO Director on an email referencing a delayed document request. This could raise a red flag during the complaints process because proper protocols were not followed.

All Investigators have been guilty of one or more of these examples during their career; however, it is a problem when this occurs on a consistent basis. All of these errors can easily be corrected, and we will suggest solutions for many of them in the forthcoming chapters.

Agency Review/Feedback:

Next, we will address the pet peeves the Agency has while reviewing ROIs produced by Investigators and submitted by Vendors.

In 2021, AES sent email inquiries to approximately 150 EEO Directors in the federal government. We offered each Director of these Agencies a chance to speak with AES about concerns they were facing, and to set a time to discuss ways to streamline the complaints process.

Below are the responses and feedback we received about the concerns with EEO Investigations.

- For a harassment case, only inquiring about incidents documented on the acceptance letter without inquiring about other potential incidents like or related to the HWE.
- Asking thorough questions about the Complainant's protected classes so an accurate decision can be made on whether they participated in prior EEO activity or qualified as a QUID.
- Not asking foundational questions or using compound questions.
- Not having a good understanding of reprisal and what constitutes the standard of reprisal.
- Asking incomplete questions that will not produce thorough responses.
- Investigators not asking enough follow-up questions.
- Not following up on gaps in testimony.
- Not following up to get a complete response to a question.
- Documents not being legible.
- Not obtaining the documents referenced in testimony.
- Neglecting to ask for and include comparator data.
- Failing to note the correct models/standards of proof.

Notice, the Vendor and Agency address some of the same concerns. Many of the concerns above were relayed multiple times but we only noted them once to reduce redundancy.

The concerns listed above will be addressed throughout this book, while instructional guidance and proven practices will be provided so professionals can improve their EEO Investigations.

Final Agency Decision (FAD) Writer/Feedback:

FAD writers are extremely cognizant of the shortcomings of EEO Investigations as they use the ROI to make a merit determination.

Many FAD writers have said the same thing, "there is no perfect ROI;" however, they express frustration when the ROI is inadequate, as that makes their job difficult. A FAD writer will send the ROI back for supplemental information, if necessary.

AES has a team of professional FAD writers who are all attorneys, and below are their responses regarding ROI concerns.

- The ROI not containing the appropriate documentation, or it contains the documentation, but it is not properly labeled or bookmarked (usually all the documents are just grouped in a single TAB without any organization) making it difficult to find and reference the documents.
- RMOs are not asked about comparators and there is no comparative data or workforce profile data in the case file.
- There is missing testimony from an RMO or witness but there is not anything in the file regarding why, so you cannot tell if it was overlooked by the Investigator or just unavailable.
- No questions were asked about the frequency/duration of actions to decide if the action(s) were consistent and pervasive enough to be considered harassment or create a hostile work environment.
- The ROI does not fully address the accepted issues, or the questioning treats dismissed claims as discrete acts.
- The Investigator fails to ask follow-up questions that are needed to address the PF elements, leaving a huge question mark over the case.

- Failure to interview a relevant witness/RMO without any justification in the record.
- Failure to obtain relevant documents without anything in the record from the Agency indicating that the record either does not exist or is unavailable.
- Questions are asked about the wrong basis/purview, or it is just missed in general, Investigators do not make sure the purview questions match the accepted claims; cut and paste is usually the culprit.
- When asking about retaliation for the instant complaint, the Investigator does not clarify that that is what they are asking about, and not other earlier EEO activity. Many RMOs will not understand that the current complaint is the basis for retaliation.
- When an RMO obviously misreads the question, the Investigator does not clarify, especially when it goes to a central issue.
- The Investigators do not make sure they are asking the right question to the right RMO (do not ask one Supervisor why he issued a reprimand when it was actually a different Supervisor who issued it. It is ok to ask what they knew about it though.)
- If CP clarified dates in their affidavit, but the Investigator does not use the clarified dates for the RMO affidavits unless CP was obviously wrong based on other evidence in the report.
- If a date is obviously wrong and it is evident that the incident occurred on a different date, but the Investigator fails to use that other date. Sometimes RMOs, because a question has the wrong dates, the RMOs have used that as an excuse to just not answer the question.

- Not managing duplicates and having the same documents in the record over and over again.
- When a 100-page policy is included with no indication of which part is relevant.
- Not asking for comparators for the disparate treatment claims.
- Having to conduct their own mini-investigations to get supplement information not obtained by the Investigator.
- Lack of experience and not knowing what is actually needed.
- The box-checking method does not cut it, but the Investigator does not have a holistic understanding of the case and where it might go.
- If the Agency makes an error and the Investigator does not should address it. **Ex:** Agency accepted failure to accommodate as an issue but did not list disability as a basis.

Again, there are many of the same concerns at this level when reviewing the ROIs. These FAD writers have provided invaluable information to which Investigators should be privy.

AES has designated chapters in this book to address some of the common concerns mentioned by these FAD writers; Comparators **(Chapter 6)** and Drafting Appropriate Questions **(Chapter 7)**.

Administrative Law Judge Concerns/Feedback:

AES has acquired insight from different AJs via EXCEL conferences, EEO trainings, project collaboration, and through professional networks.

Here are a few key concerns that AJs have with ROIs.

- Missing relevant witnesses
- Not obtaining affidavits from Complainant's witnesses
- Not interviewing all relevant participants in a non-selection case
- Poorly drafted questions often leading to incomplete or yes or no answers.
- Not asking follow-up questions when reviewing responses to interrogatories
- Cases missing relevant documentary evidence.
- Referring to people as RMO or Witness which causes confusion of identity.
- Sanitizing pertinent information
- Using incomplete information to determine reprisal claim.
- Lacking comparative information
- Not covering or investigating like or related incidents of harassment mentioned by the Complainant.

Some key concerns were mentioned continuously by professionals, and the basis of reprisal was a common theme. Therefore, AES has designated an entire chapter that will be an instructional example for drafting an ROI summary on a reprisal basis.

The pet peeves with EEO Investigations can be attributed to many things. We believe the common concerns can be effectively resolved. This chapter is one of the first steps towards improvement, as we have presented actual problems from stakeholders that need to be addressed.

In addition, we believe Investigators require resources for practical training so they can obtain the necessary skill sets to conduct effective EEO Investigations.

When Investigators are provided guidance and industry-proven solutions, they will be able to implement these practices in their work. We know through experience that only dedicated professionals willing to acquire the proper skills through practical training or detailed instruction will be able to address all the above-referenced concerns effectively.

Our intent is to inform EEO professionals with practical instructions and assist with what is required to successfully conduct EEO investigations. To do this effectively, we now need to provide insight into what EEO professionals encounter during an investigation. The next chapter will provide an in-depth look through the actual obstacles that an EEO Investigator faces.

CHAPTER 3

Industry Obstacles

"Conducting EEO investigations is akin to the life of a lone wolf. When I started my career as an EEO Investigator, I quickly realized there was minimal technical support, mentorship, or a sounding board. I chose to self-educate and made it a habit to review five appellate cases daily, made mock scenarios, and went to the library to practice drafting questions about all the theories of discrimination and employment actions. I had hands-on training to work on my interviewing skills, while my wife pretended to be the Complainant and respond to my verbal interrogatories. There was so much to learn, and I was determined to prepare myself before I received my first case"

> *"There is no better training than hands on experience"*

AES facilitates hundreds of EEO Investigations a year. We receive daily inquiries from Investigators looking for solutions as they face obstacles or issues that need to be addressed.

These verbatim inquiries from Investigators provide invaluable insight into real circumstances and challenges an Investigator will likely encounter and should master to be effective in their role. You will notice there is some uncertainty or lack of confidence in many responses; some inquiries show a lack of knowledge of protocols, while others are just looking for a sounding board and know exactly what they are doing.

Below, we will address the obstacles relayed by the Investigator, and AES will provide commentary.

Investigator: "Should I let my POC know that some items remain outstanding and give them five days to produce, or should I do nothing?"

Critique: The Investigator is unsure of the Agency protocols and is reluctant to take action to obtain data. These are some primary responsibilities of a neutral fact-finder.

Investigator: "CP identified an additional incident of harassment which occurred after she filed her complaint on 2/25/20. Do I need to direct her to amend her complaint to add this, or can I investigate it?"

Critique: The Investigator is unsure of EEO protocols and how to handle additional claims raised during the investigative stage. On a positive note, they asked when they were unsure of the answer.

Investigator: "I sent the Complainant the 15-day letter with 2/19 as the start date. Can I go ahead and send RMO testimony to him for rebuttal, or no since I do not have his affidavit back signed?"

Critique: The Investigator is unsure of the situation and decides to ask. We believe the Investigator knows what to do but just wants some reassurance. **Note:** This is a common inquiry.

Investigator: "I was able to get this person's contact info. As far as the questions on his affidavit. Should I just ask him the standard questions regarding his position title, name, etc., and leave out the Complainant biases questions since he does not know the Complainant?"

Critique: There is a typo in this inquiry which can cause confusion, "biases or basis." Another concern here is with the Investigator assuming someone does not know the Complainant. Also, based on specific agency protocols, the Investigator should know if protected classes should be asked for individuals who are not RMOs.

Investigator: "On the document request feedback it states, "Two-year comparative data for harassment needed." I'm not sure what data is being referred to?"

Critique: Investigators should obtain two-year data for harassment complaints filed against the relevant RMOs. The Investigator was not familiar with this requirement; however, it is a standard request asked by seasoned Investigators.

Investigator: "There are a couple of RMOs who were listed in the counselor's report of the administrative file, but after obtaining their affidavits, they have almost no information related to the accepted issue. How do I proceed with including their affidavit?

1. Do I write up a summary of their testimony and include it with my ROI?
2. Do I write up a memo regarding their testimony but don't include it in my ROI?"

Critique: This Investigator is experienced, and what they are addressing comes down to Agency preference. They are checking in to make sure before acting, but they know exactly what to do.

Investigator: "In my case, she has a union rep who is very hands-on. All that is left for CP to do is a rebuttal opportunity. (Just FYI They have objected to due dates from the start because CP does not do anything without the representative walking through it with her). I received an email from the rep that after having three strokes back-to-back (before I received the case) she is now on emergency medical leave until April 1. I just did not know if that made any difference as far as the due date, or any extension. I am just not certain of the "role" of the union representative in a situation like this. Please advise. I know CP will resist when I send her rebuttal opportunity, so I wanted to know going in how to handle it."

Critique: The Investigator is not thinking for themselves or does not have the experience in dealing with this type of situation. **Note:** This is a learning experience for this Investigator.

Investigator: "This is an AWOL/termination case. The CP, when asked who she is comparing herself to (whether others have been treated more favorably), provides several names. I want to confirm that I do not need to interview these people, but rather that I can ask the RMO the following: CP alleges that Joe Smith white male, was treated more favorably in that he was not charged AWOL or terminated while on probation. Is this true, yes, or no? Please explain fully."

Critique: This Investigator is experienced, what they are asking is based on Agency preferences. Some Agencies want all alleged comparators to be interviewed, others only if testimony will clarify if they are a comparator or not.

Investigator: "The responses are trickling in, and they either are corroborating CPs statements he was harassed, or they claim they don't know anything. It's getting down to the wire on this one. Do you think I should interview more of the witnesses he provided? I have obtained the testimony of 8 of his 18 identified witnesses. He claimed all of them could attest to the alleged discrimination and harassment; about three have claimed they have not witnessed any harassment."

Critique: This Investigator is inexperienced in dealing with numerous interviews/deadlines. There are specific tactics that can be utilized to qualify witnesses given the limited time frame, but it is clear the Investigator is panicked, and not in control.

Investigator: "I have the SF-50s for Mary Poppins and Robin Hood showing that they resigned from the Agency. I have home addresses that may or may not be current so I could send a letter asking if they would give an affidavit, but I can't say I think it's worth the effort."

Critique: The Investigator knows the protocol for contacting retired federal employees.

Investigator: "How do I identify who the appropriate Management official(s) should be when a complainant resigns and files a constructive discharge claim? Do I just obtain statements from all Supervisors in the complainant's chain of command ie. First, second, and third-line Supervisors?"

Critique: The Investigator did not have experience with this type of complaint, nor do many. Research into constructive discharge was conducted, and the Investigator focused on a harassment purview. This is a good example of a professional Investigator.

Investigator: "The RMO for Drexal is retired, so to my knowledge, no longer required to participate in this stage of the investigation. How do we handle this? He mentioned his mother also recently passed and stated clearly, he is not available."

Critique: This Investigator understands the protocol for retired employees participating but has forgotten that utilization of an MTF can effectively address this circumstance for the record.

Investigator: "In the case file, the RMO did state the CP is not allowed a promotion while in non-contact status, so would it be necessary to ask policy questions related to promotion and non-contact status, since the RMO has mentioned it?"

Critique: This Investigator has uncertainty of relevance but shows good attention to detail.

Investigator: "Do we need to notify the Agency when Complainant has elected to have an attorney representative during the course of an investigation? Or do we have a designation or Representative form to include in the record?"

Critique: This Investigator is unclear on the Agency's protocols for updating the Designation of Representation but understands the importance of the election, and that it must be part of the record.

Investigator: "I have a quick question for you. Does the Agency require that we ask all affiants, including SMEs and miscellaneous witnesses, whether they were aware of the Complainant's protected classes? Does this apply even to whether they had knowledge of Complainant's disability? I always have in the past with cases, but I am a bit hesitant asking whether a witness was aware of the Complainant's disability status."

Critique: This is an experienced Investigator who does not know the Agency's preference pertaining to disclosures of protected information. Note: This has become a common inquiry.

Investigator: "They provided rescinded copies of the facility policy for EEO and Harassment. Do you think we should obtain their current facility EEO and Harassment policy?"

Critique: The Investigator is uncertain; they understand what they have been provided is not sufficient but need reassurance.

Investigator: "Agency produced documents, but some are still outstanding. How do I address this, or should I simply draft a Memo to the File, the documents were not provided?"

Critique: The Investigator is not familiar with the Agency's protocols for escalation.

Investigator: I have a quick question for you. On 2/19, Complainant sent me his draft responses to the interview questions. We then spoke on 2/24 for the actual interview and I sent his statement to him for review/signing on 2/26. I have sent him reminder emails on 3/2 and 3/4. Complainant replied on 3/5 apologizing for the delay stating that he had been sick and would get it to me ASAP. However, to date, I have not received it. I am sending him another reminder email and following up with a phone call today. My question is if there is no response, do I need to send him a 15-day letter for not returning the signed affidavit? And in the event that he does not return it when it comes time for me to submit my ROI, do I include the unsigned version with an MTF? Please advise, thank you."

Critique: The Investigator is uncertain about what to do and is not confident about the protocols for compliance or properly documenting the record, but they seem to understand what is appropriate.

Investigator: In the Johnson case, CP is represented by an attorney. I emailed her but it bounced back, stating the email address is no longer valid. I called and left a message. From what I can gather she left the firm she was with and is working on her own. If she doesn't call me back by Tuesday, may I call CP or have my POC call CP to inquire about her attorney and connect with the attorney?"

Critique: This is an experienced Investigator who is resourceful and knowledgeable about attorney/client communication.

Investigator: "How should I respond to CPs attorney's question below? This is the second time he has asked me if he can draft RMO questions. The first time I told him I already had them drafted and appreciated his offer, but now he's asking me again."

Critique: The Investigator is experienced, but dealing with a pushy attorney so they want reassurance on how to handle the situation.

EEO Investigators have a tough job! Many of the obstacles the Investigators faced were not based on EEO laws or theory, but rather Statement of Work/Performance Work Statement protocols, dealing with various personalities, and non-compliance issues.

This proves that there is no better training than hands-on experience.

The examples above deliver the truth about the required technical knowledge, attention to detail, and experience it takes to conduct EEO Investigations. To navigate through the investigative stage, there are specific practical skills that will help the Investigator be successful. We will discuss these practical skills in the next few chapters, with detailed examples and instructions.

CHAPTER 4

Practical Skills (Professional)

There are practical skills necessary to conduct EEO Investigations. Professionals must have or acquire both professional and technical skills to be successful. This chapter will focus on basic **professional skills** that Investigators should hone.

Examples, tactics, and scenarios for each skill will be provided and will address the benefits or consequences of not using certain practical skills.

Proofreading: An efficient way to eliminate typos is to draft multiple pre-written communications for common email correspondences.

Example: Hello Mr. Heath, my name is Gary Smith, and I am your assigned EEO Investigator. I am reaching out to introduce myself, schedule a time to answer questions you may have about the formal complaint process, and set up date/time for a telephonic interview.

Crafting the email above eliminates typos, and errors, and saves the Investigator time when facilitating multiple cases. Sometimes Investigators are going through the motions with administrative duties, and they need a foolproof way to mitigate the burnout, multiple responsibilities, or other distractions. The benefit of sending out pre-written communications is that the Investigator will always be sending out professional correspondence that is clear and free of typos.

Failing to properly proofread and find a way to eliminate typos in correspondences and on work products will send a message that the Investigator is not professional, or serious about their role. Too many careless typos can bring credibility into question, even when the professional has years of practical hands-on experience. Think about this situation: If someone were in court, and their Lawyer spelled their name incorrectly on official court documents and used poor grammar, what thoughts would cross their mind about the services they would be receiving during their trial?

Typos are plentiful in EEO matters; they are on acceptance letters, affidavits, ROIs, and emails. Professionals should always make the extra effort to eliminate typos during the EEO Investigation.

Timely: The phrase being on "Military time" is not much to ask of a professional. Successful EEO Investigators do not procrastinate; they are highly efficient at accomplishing multiple tasks promptly. Prioritizing responsibilities is the key to good time management.

Example: The Investigator has the following tasks they need to complete: (1) ROI draft due in three days which they need to start. (2) IP/DR due in 24/48 hours. (3) An interview in an hour. Which task should they prioritize first, so all can be completed in a timely manner?

How an Investigator assesses their responsibilities, deadlines, and the necessary time it takes to complete each task, will either keep them organized or cause them to miss deadlines. We will analyze each responsibility and discuss how it should be prioritized.

ROI due: If the draft ROI is due in three days for review, the Investigator is already behind schedule since they have not started drafting the report. With three days left to submittal, they should be proofreading their work. Summarizing affidavits immediately after interviews is beneficial. When the details and context of the complaint are fresh in the Investigator's memory, it helps them determine if supplemental information is needed. If additional testimony is necessary, there is plenty of time as opposed to if they found insufficient testimony three days prior to their due date.

IP/DR: (Due in 24/48hrs) How many issues does the acceptance letter have? Does the Investigator prefer to work on a task until it is completed? Could the IP/DR be completed in under one hour? Or how about, complete 50% and finish it later? This task should not take more than one or two hours at most. It is ultimately whatever works best for the Investigator, but we recommend that they do not feel rushed to finish as this could affect the quality.

An interview in 1 hour: How long does the Investigator anticipate this call to be? Are they prepared for the call? Do they have the questions pulled up? Do they have the phone number they will call? Have they eaten? Gone to the bathroom? Checked their email for responses that need to be addressed immediately. Can the Investigator coordinate all of this within an hour prior to the call? Be organized and on time! Investigators need to be 100% focused during their interviews, not distracted by searching for documents, a growling stomach, full bladder, and email pings

(putting out fires before the call will keep Investigators from being distracted during the call, or curious to check their emails.)

AES's recommendation: Given the scenario, we would recommend preparing for the call that will take place in an hour. After the call, complete the IP/DR and then focus on writing the ROI for the next two and a half days. There is no correct answer, but the best method is to prioritize responsibilities to ensure deadlines can be met.

Flexibility: In an EEO Investigation, matters rarely go according to plan. EEO Investigations require Investigators to improvise and make themselves available to take advantage of opportunities.

Example: When investigating claims, I used to conduct interviews on the spot without a scheduled appointment, no morning coffee, or I would put aside whatever task I was performing.

I was always ready and available under any circumstance for the following reasons. That person was being deployed in three weeks, going to the hospital for surgery, going on vacation, or just impossible to reach in general because of their job responsibilities. Investigators should always be ready to execute! I would sometimes have to write testimony or details on napkins, post-it notes, random objects, in pencil, pen, or Sharpie, then later type on an affidavit. There were times when I held conversations in the following settings: sitting in the car with no A/C, walking around a restaurant to find reception, waiting rooms, family dinner table, and so on just so I could get the information I needed for a case.

Investigators must be flexible and do what is necessary given the circumstances, or the case could be delayed and untimely. There will be times when they miss meals, eat at their desk, or get caught on a long call and need to use the restroom. Being flexible can be uncomfortable but it is necessary at times. Fortunately, it is not the norm.

> *Example: The Investigator is working on an ROI that is due, and they have no other plans for the day. Everything is going according to plan, and then their email pings. Do they check it? Their phone rings, it is a person they have been trying to reach for a week to get testimony. Do they answer it? There is a knock on their front door. Do they go and answer it, or focus on completing the ROI?*

Over the years, we have seen Investigators miss important opportunities for not being available. They have missed opportunities for new cases by not being responsive to emails, missed important calls that required immediate attention, and had packages arrive containing signed affidavits and requested documents marked as "undeliverable" for not being available to sign for the package. Being flexible and ready ensures EEO Investigations are completed with all pertinent information in a timely manner.

Listening: Every investigation will contain *some* human error. There might be an occasional date that is incorrect, claims not stated accurately, names misspelled, etc. However, paying attention to detail is vital and is the difference between an investigation that is sufficient and one that may be remanded for supplemental information. Listening is the key to asking pertinent

follow-up questions during an interview so the correct information can be documented.

Example: Sally filed a claim based on race and age, and while she is describing the events that took place, she mentions that Management chastised her because she filed a complaint against them.

If the Investigator is listening to what Sally relays, she is mentioning/alleging reprisal for a complaint she filed against Management. However, prior EEO activity is not mentioned as one of the protected classes.

There are follow-up questions the Investigator needs to ask to verify and assess Sally's testimony, see below.

Question: What type of complaint did you file against these Management officials? How would they have known you filed this complaint, and when?

Question: Are you alleging reprisal for prior EEO activity or opposition?

Question: Do you want to add prior EEO activity as one of your protected classes to this complaint?

If Sally wants to add prior EEO activity as a protected class, the Investigator can then explain Sally's right to do so during the investigative stage. Now, the purview of reprisal will be covered. Sally is relieved and grateful because this information was noted on her formal complaint form and the Investigator has made it possible for her to update her complaint.

Example: Sally is now excited and mentions there were other things omitted that were on her formal complaint form. She goes into detail about events, dates, and other claims.

While listening to Sally, the Investigator realizes the events Sally is speaking of were captured on the acceptance letter but misstated, according to Sally. The Investigator explains to Sally that there is a specific time period noted on the acceptance letter to address concerns with incidents that are misstated or not worded correctly.

While listening to Sally, the Investigator realizes the dates Sally is speaking of are untimely and were dismissed in the acceptance letter. However, these claims will be covered as background information under the hostile work environment purview.

Additionally, the Investigator noticed the other claims were not in the Counseling Report, nor the formal intake form. The Investigator explains to Sally that she will need to contact the EEO office if she wishes to amend her complaint with additional claims.

The Investigator's primary job responsibility is to identify and collect pertinent information for the record. Effective listening results in appropriate actions that potentially reduce delays, remands, supplemental inquiries, and possible sanctions for the Agency.

Forthrightness: Passive personality types will have a challenging time managing control during EEO Investigations. The investigative process is supposed to be a non-adversarial process, but every side has its own agenda so there will be

disagreements and confrontations at times. Representatives and attorneys for the Complainant who are savvy, aggressive, and pushy could view the Investigator as a pushover if they do not stand their ground when appropriate.

Investigators must convey their responsibility as neutral fact-finders and take control of the investigation in a straightforward manner. Investigators should be self-confident, not submissive when faced with confrontation. They should arm themselves with some tough skin to keep control and conduct a neutral investigation.

Attorneys are skilled in trying to present their client's side of the story as being the truth. They will try to control the investigation, and some are crafty, or sit back and wait for an error during the investigative stage. Some will dictate unreasonable demands to burden the process. They are forthright in their responsibilities to protect their client; it is not their intent to be neutral.

> *Example: Complainant's attorney says they cannot provide the client's signed affidavit because he (the Attorney) will be in court for the next three weeks on trial for another case.*

The attorney has let the Investigator know what their priority is, and it is not the Investigator's priority to get the Complainant's signed affidavit.

What should the Investigator say, in response? "Ok, thanks please provide at your convenience." Or should they respond, "Would your client like to extend the investigative period if a signed affidavit cannot be provided within 15 days?" Or could they email the attorney a 15-day Non-Compliance letter?

In a situation such as this, we would suggest sending the attorney a 15-day Non-Compliance letter. They may not like it, but they have to respect the action.

> *Example: Complainant is not providing direct questions to the Investigator's interrogatories. The Investigator asks Complainant why the Supervisor downgraded him, and he says, "Because I am a male." The Investigator asks Complainant for witnesses, and he says, "I don't have names." The Investigator asks him why they were downgraded, and he responds, "Refer to the official letter."*

Should the Investigator accept these answers as the Complainant's testimony? Or should the Investigator reiterate/reword the questions to possibly get a different response? Would it be more effective to ask follow-up questions to get detailed responses? If the Investigator still receives the same responses, what should they do? Should they draft a Memorandum to the File documenting their attempts to obtain testimony or is it appropriate to tell the Complainant his responses are incomplete and need more detail? What method or tactics should the Investigator use to get the information required for the record, and when do they stop inquiring?

Investigators have deadlines, and there are protocols for the investigative process as well as compliance statutes. During an Investigation, it is imperative at times to use some statutes or compliance measures. Some of these methods will make the recipient mad, flustered, or retaliatory. Investigators must be direct about the information they need to acquire during the investigative stage. The consequence of not being forthright is that multiple professionals in the process could take advantage of them, including the Complainant or his attorney, EEO Office staff, RMOs, Witnesses, and even the Vendor that is paying them for their services. If Investigators are direct, follow the correct protocols, and have good interpersonal skills, they will be able to interact effectively to meet the requirements of conducting a sound EEO investigation.

Interpersonal skills: Strong communication skills are necessary as more than 70% of conducting EEO Investigations involves dealing with people, and 50% of that involves interviewing individuals. We do not believe it necessary to be an extreme extrovert, but Investigators generally need to enjoy working with people. To effectively communicate, emotional intelligence is necessary to assess the different personalities, egos, and emotions that manifest. It is vital to understand when it is the right time to listen, show empathy, or be assertive.

Example: The Investigator calls the Agency to follow up about delayed documents. The EEO Specialist answers the phone call but sounds a bit down. How should the Investigator assess this situation? Do they tell the EEO Specialist this is the third time reaching out to her office? Or do they ask if everything is ok, and spend some time getting to know someone that they are working with on a case?

Investigators should get to know the people they are working and interacting with in this process. At the right time, they should find something in common, genuinely inquire about how that person is doing, and truly listen. Being aggressive or pushy is not always the best approach, only sometimes does "the squeaky wheel get the oil."

Example: The Investigator picks up the phone call and the Complainant is venting about the EEO process, the EEO office, past Investigators, and giving off bad energy. How should the Investigator handle this situation? Should they cut the Complainant off and tell them to schedule a call at another date and time? Do they tell them they have nothing to do with that, and that they are a neutral third party? Should the Investigator just sit back and listen? Should the Investigators start defending themselves and others from the allegations being made?

The purpose of the EEO process is to address discrimination, but some Complainants use the process to vent their frustrations as well. We have experienced Complainants who have filed complaints hoping that someone would just listen, they have no intention other than to be heard. Our Counselors would encounter this at the informal stage, where the Aggrieved Person was seeking no remedy other than wanting leadership to know what was going on. Taking some time out of the day to listen may actually resolve the underlying problem. Effectively dealing with the Complainant under these circumstances brings the Investigator one step closer to conducting an effective EEO investigation.

Example: During a call, an RMO is giving the Investigator a hard time and being uncooperative, yelling at them, making rude remarks, threatening to report the Investigator, and cursing in an unprofessional manner. How should the Investigator handle the situation? Do they defend themselves, prove they have more power than the RMO, and put them in their place with their knowledge of EEO law? Do they tuck their tail and say "Yes sir, Yes Ma'am? Should the Investigator apologize, and adjust the way they approach the hostility, so they do not add "fuel to the fire"? Should they tell the RMO they will disconnect if they continue to be unprofessional?

Investigators should never be pushovers. However, others may test their knowledge, patience, or boundaries throughout the investigation. There is no blueprint for dealing with people, but it is important to understand when someone is crossing the line and let them know that in a professional way. Yelling, humiliating, and cursing back at the person is not professional and will likely steer the investigation off course. Investigators need to be flexible and accommodating, and adjust their approach to difficult people and situations. Sometimes that requires being assertive and direct about their thoughts and actions, as well as reminding the other person about the objective of the investigation and that the Investigator is a neutral party. Investigators need to control how they react to these types of conflicts so they can respond in an effective way.

Attitude: How do others in the process view the person conducting the Investigation? It is rare for anyone to physically see the Investigator except for onsite interviews or through video conferences. It is difficult to assess nonverbal cues, however, those involved in the process do notice the way the Investigator handles themselves during interviews, calls, and through email communication. Does the Investigator appear professional,

organized, and experienced or does he seem incompetent, anxious, and unqualified?

Example: The Complainant asks the Investigator by email what they can expect during the EEO process.

Investigator response #1: I will interview you and others and put my findings in a report.

Investigator response #2: I will explain during our interview in detail. Please prepare your questions.

Investigator response #3: I will take your testimony by phone or through interrogatories, ask for witnesses, and collect any evidence you have based on your accepted issues. I will then interview relevant Management officials about the accepted claims. You will be provided with a chance to rebut their statements. If you have any questions during the investigative period, please reach out to me so I can answer them.

Investigator response #4: If an attorney represents you, I will let them go over the details of the process with you. If you are not represented, you can research on www.eeoc.gov for details on the formal complaint process.

None of the responses from the Investigator are "wrong," but some are stronger than others and some convey a specific attitude of the Investigator. An Investigator must be conscious of the words they choose and how they come across. This will affect how people respond and interact with them during the complaint process.

Example: *The Complainant calls the Investigator and asks why all their (Complainant's) witnesses have not been contacted for an interview.*

Investigator response #1: *I do not have contact information for all of them; can you provide it at your convenience?*

Investigator response #2: *I interviewed those who were relevant to the claim; is there anyone else you suggest that is relevant to the claim? If so, tell me to what they can attest.*

Investigator response #3: *I make the decision on who to interview. It is the Investigator's discretion.*

Investigator response #4: *When you provided the witnesses, you did not explain what they could attest to, so I used my discretion when choosing who to interview.*

Investigator response #5: *I interviewed 5 out of 10; they all said the same thing.*

Investigators have used the above responses to address the same inquiry from a Complainant. Some Investigators get annoyed with the Complainant's demands and provide a response that can be misconstrued as rude, condescending, or accusatory. A proper response to this inquiry from the Investigator will hold the Complainant responsible and adequately address the matter in a professional manner.

Example: *There were multiple witnesses provided, and I asked each one of them what they could attest to so I used my discretion to assess if their testimony would provide evidence or is relevant to your claim of discrimination based on your protected class. There is one other person*

I would like to reach out to, but I need updated contact information. Could you please provide that information?

> **Example: During the interview, the Complainant asked the Investigator if it made sense to add background information even though it was not accepted as a claim.**

Investigator response #1: I am a neutral third party, I cannot assist.

Investigator response #2: I am not your representative nor the attorney which you hired; I cannot provide advice to you.

Investigator response #3: You need to address that with the EEO office.

Investigator response #4: Listen, off the record, you should because I think it's relevant.

Investigator response #5: Anything you believe is relevant to your complaint can be addressed during your testimony.

Investigator response #6: It is your case; you can provide whatever information you desire. It does not guarantee it will be considered unless it is relevant.

It is appropriate for an Investigator to let the Complainant know their role as an Investigator, and what they can and cannot discuss. It is all about the manner in which they respond. The Investigator can absolutely address a Complainant's rights and responsibilities during the investigative process, and some of the responses above relay that information.

It is important for Investigators to choose their words wisely to exhibit an appropriate attitude for dealing with circumstances or questions that come up during the formal complaint process.

Accountability: All Investigators make mistakes and must treat them as a lesson rather than a blow to their ego. In this industry, Investigators are respected for acknowledging their errors rather than always trying to be correct and prove their point. If Investigators take accountability for their errors and learn from a situation, they will be provided with additional opportunities whereas Investigators that are combative and never take responsibility for their mistakes will be given less work.

Example: The Investigator puts the wrong case number on the ROI, they forget to investigate all the accepted issues, and they reference the wrong protected class throughout the ROI. What would be the best response or action?

Response/Action #1: They make excuses about their personal life and the same errors occur in future cases.

Response/Action #2: I do not see any issues; everything looks fine to me. They continue to hold their position on the matter until the evidence is pointed out and no longer debatable.

Response/Action #3: They do not respond at all, no longer return email messages, and abandon their case(s).

Response/Action #4: They do not say anything, and they make the necessary changes to the file.

Response/Action #5: They say, "I don't know how that happened; it will never happen again," and they make the appropriate changes moving forward.

Response/Action #6: They admit they messed up, try to figure out what went wrong, and make the appropriate changes moving forward.

These are all real responses and actions we hear when ROIs are deemed insufficient. Investigators improve when they take accountability and are open to feedback. Being receptive to constructive criticism allows them to receive relevant guidance on how to improve. This is part of the growth process to becoming a successful EEO Investigator. If an Investigator is always defensive and cannot handle feedback, they will struggle, and opportunities will be limited as people will not want to work with them.

All of the skills named in this chapter are basic and useful for many industries. We have specifically shown, through realistic scenarios, how these **basic** skills are **essential** skills. These are some of the **key** practical skills that allow an Investigator to be effective during the investigative stage.

The next chapter will focus on technical skills that help the Investigator to produce a quality ROI.

CHAPTER 5

Practical Skills (Technical)

Conducting EEO Investigations requires much more than general knowledge of EEO law. Investigators must understand Employment Law as a foundation, however, there are skills required to apply the knowledge effectively. This chapter will cover the specific skills and tactics that need to be refined. These are the practical skills or "how-tos" that an EEO Investigator should master to be successful.

Comparators:

This is one of the hardest things for Investigators to grasp; therefore, we have designated an entire chapter **(Chapter 6)** to cover the nuances of this topic. This is a game changer when it comes to the quality of EEO Investigations. Even seasoned Investigators contact us from time to time to go over comparator scenarios.

Note: A true comparator is a person similarly situated to the Complainant, who has a different protected class than Complainant, and did not experience the same treatment or action as Complainant.

What does that mean, and how does the Investigator find a comparator? Let's go over this below:

Situation: The Supervisor "Bob" decides he will be providing overtime to only half of his employees. When the overtime list is posted, all the employees who did not receive overtime are upset because of the lost opportunity for additional money. However, some of these employees also feel they have been discriminated against. All the employees that received overtime are male, except for one (1), who is a female. The employees that were not selected for overtime are all women.

Here are some questions to ponder: Does it appear there could be discrimination in this situation? Does something seem wrong or off? Is there more information that is missing? Who would be a comparator in this situation? What information or evidence should the Investigator try to obtain for the record? Why were mostly males provided overtime and not the females?

Identifying a true comparator takes skill and a good understanding of three key elements:

(1) Who is ideally similarly situated?
(2) Who had a different employment action? and
(3) Who had a different protected class?

Let's go over a few details for each of these key elements and break down this situation.

Similarly situated: It appears all the employees are working under Bob, because it says, "half of his employees." Does this mean they are all similarly situated? What if they have different position titles and duties? What if some of the employees are full-time and others part-time? What if some are FTEs and others are contractors?

All these factors and others should be considered until the Investigator can reasonably identify an employee as being similarly situated. The Investigator should look for employees that mirror Complainant. To assist in finding a similarly situated person, the Investigator should request a workforce profile for the unit in which the Complainant works. This workforce profile should document all employees under Bob's supervision, broken down by unit, position title, grade, and employment status.

Let's look at the next key element - different employment actions.

Employment Action: The Complainant for this claim was not provided overtime. This is easy, the Investigator needs to identify employees that had a different employment action. This means identifying those that were selected for overtime. The Investigator can request a list of employees, during the time in question, which were selected for overtime by the Supervisor, Bob.

Let's look at the third key element.

Protected Class: The Complainant for this claim is a female. This should also be easy; the Investigator needs to identify employees that are male. The Investigator should ask that the list of names for the people that were provided overtime by Bob, to be annotated by sex.

When the Investigator receives the requested information from the Agency, they can determine if there are any potential comparators, by understanding the three key elements we addressed.

Identifying comparators is a requirement for all EEO Investigations excluding a denied reasonable accommodation claim.

Witnesses:

Investigations should not contain hearsay testimony; relevant witnesses should be identified and deposed. Key witnesses have direct evidence of discrimination or intent. Relevant witnesses may have been involved in an employment action, possessing detailed information that could provide circumstantial evidence. Not everyone is a viable witness just because someone names or labels them as such.

> *Example: Complainant tells the Investigator, "Interview Mr. John Smith, he can tell all about the hostile work environment. I always informed him about my harassment, and he saw that I was flustered immediately after speaking to my supervisor."*

The example above is not an example of a strong witness. If someone proposes a witness, questions should be asked to assess if they are a witness with relevant information.

Below are some questions that help identify witnesses to be interviewed.

Question: Did Mr. John Smith witness the events you allege were harassment? If so, explain how he was in the position to witness?

Question: Is there anyone who has knowledge that your sex was the reason for the harassment? What information do you think they will attest to?

Question: *Were there any people that were first-hand witnesses to these events? If so, explain how they were in a position to witness?*

It is an important skill for an Investigator to be able to identify, clarify, and ask appropriate questions to gather direct and circumstantial evidence from witnesses.

There will be times when a Complainant names 20 witnesses, the RMOs name 10 witnesses, and the Investigator identifies five potential witnesses to be interviewed. That would be a lot of witnesses to interview. Remember, only relevant witnesses should be interviewed. Using some of the questions presented above will clarify who may have relevant evidence for the record.

Keynote: If a proposed witness is not interviewed, a memorandum to the file should be drafted on the reason the Investigator made that decision.

Interviewing all key witnesses or making reasonable attempts to obtain testimony will result in sufficient ROI. However, not interviewing or not documenting the reason(s) for not interviewing witnesses will result in a deficient ROI.

Keynote: If the Investigator is unsure if someone is a witness, they should err on the side of caution and interview them.

The skill of identifying witnesses is imperative. This skill can be successfully implemented by asking the questions and adhering to the keynotes addressed.

Interviewing Skills:

Introducing oneself as the Investigator, what to say?

Should an Investigator consider what they would say to an affiant prior to scheduling an interview with them? Has the Investigator rehearsed an introduction, visualized the dialogue, or thought about what message they might leave on a voicemail? It is important that the Investigator is prepared to introduce themselves in a polished manner. Professional first impressions when speaking to affiants during the EEO process are vital.

An EEO investigation is a serious and personal matter for the Complainant and those accused of discrimination allegations. The Investigator has the responsibility of facilitating the process in a professional manner.

> **Ex: "Jill, it's Frank your EEO Investigator. I need to interview you ASAP. Call me."**

The correspondence above achieves the goal of the EEO Investigator, but what will the Complainant (Jill) or anyone else involved in the EEO process think about the Investigator's correspondence?

Investigators do not have to make friends with everyone with whom they interact, but they should take caution in how they communicate with everyone involved in the formal complaint process. Look at Frank's correspondence; should anything be changed or is Frank getting off to a good start?

Ex: "Hello Jill, my name is Frank Berstein. I am the assigned Investigator for your formal complaint of discrimination. I am reaching out to introduce myself and set up a date/time for an interview."

The above example is professional, is a great first impression, and provides details on the next step in the process.

Etiquette for interviewing affiants

1. **Neutral:**
   Remain neutral, whether an affiant's statement seems plausible or not. The Investigator's purview is to gather testimony and facts relevant to the case. When speaking to an affiant, the Investigator should make sure not to come across as biased. The Investigator should see every statement presented as an allegation and not a fact. If something does not make sense or is vague, Investigators should ask for clarification or present follow-up questions rather than assuming.

2. **Timeliness:**
   Investigators should be respectful of an affiant's time and make sure affiants are respectful of theirs. Investigators should always provide a window or agree on a time that can be met even when unforeseen delays occur. Be prompt in responding to emails and sending material to affiants that are requested. Investigators should make sure they follow up in a timely manner, especially when emails go unanswered in reference to setting up interviews.

3. **Patience:**
   Not all affiants will be available to speak with Investigators on a certain date. Investigators need to accommodate affiants' schedules and allow them ample time to provide a convenient date for an interview. Investigators should not rush an affiant through the questions or the interview process. They should take time and provide affiants with the time to answer the questions being presented. Everyone has a different communication style; at times, the Investigator must adjust their desired communication style, so the interview process is smooth for the affiant.

4. **Reiteration:**
   Investigators should not become annoyed if an affiant does not provide an answer to a question they ask repeatedly, either ask again slowly or find another way to ask the same question. After a statement or response is provided to a question, the Investigator should reiterate what they heard to clarify if the affiant agrees with what will be documented as their response on the affidavit.

5. **Empathy:**
   Investigators are not confidants for the affiants; however, they should be aware people will get emotional and tell them personal matters. They should make sure they are respectful of affiants' feelings. For example, Investigators should not keep asking questions if someone is in the middle of crying; they could simply say "It's ok, take your time." The EEO process can be incredibly stressful and hard for affiants. Investigators need to let them know the process can be stressful and the Investigator is there to walk them through it.

6. Professionalism:

Investigators should be in control of the process and facilitate it accordingly. They should mind their manners, as respect is earned through the knowledge and professionalism they display. They should not go off on a "power trip" and demand things; they can simply ask and say, "Could you please provide this? I would appreciate it." Investigators should refrain from being too casual with affiants. Sometimes a humorous topic/circumstance may come up, but Investigators should not make a habit of joking or laughing during their interviews.

Patience:

There will be delays during EEO Investigations when dealing with people and life situations happen. However, there is incompetence, haphazardness, and procrastination. A lot of EEO cases are delayed by waiting around for someone else to do something. To mitigate delays, Investigators must be flexible and move forward without tasks getting done in a logical order. This could mean supplementing affidavits, inserting placeholders for documents, or drafting an ROI with incomplete sections.

Example: After two weeks of the Investigator trying to obtain testimony, the Complainant has not responded. The case is not moving forward, and the Investigator is frustrated trying to chase down the Complainant and hearing one excuse after another.

Example: The RMO promised to send his signed affidavit, which is necessary to provide a rebuttal opportunity. The Investigator is annoyed because their deadline for the ROI is approaching.

Example: The investigation is complete, everyone is interviewed, and the Agency has not provided any of the documents that were requested

45 days ago. Every time the Investigator sends an email to the EEO Specialist, they respond "I'm on it" or they get an out-of-office message. The Investigator is aggravated because they cannot complete their ROI without the documents.

Example: *A key witness in the case is no longer a federal employee, but says they are interested in providing testimony. They have no obligation to participate, and they do not have a desire to work within a reasonable turnaround time for inclusion of their testimony. The Investigator is frustrated because this testimony would be the "nail in the coffin" to cover the applicable purview.*

What should the Investigator do? Should they just wait around until people are available for testimony or inquire to find out the true reasons for the delay? Should they send a demand letter? Could they move forward without testimony and interview others in the process? Will they escalate matters to Supervisors? How about venting to whomever will listen, and hope that works? Should they start sending multiple follow-up emails, pestering, or borderline harassing people to get what they need?

There is no one choice for every situation. The Investigator must relax and assess the situation to determine the best action. Below are some examples of what could occur based on the Investigator's actions if they are patient.

Action/Reaction: *The Investigator informs the POC they are unable to reach the CP, and the POC reveals that the Complainant is in the hospital. Therefore, the POC says we can possibly get an extension to extend the investigative period.*

Action/Reaction: *The Investigator informs the Vendor with whom they contract that they are unable to obtain the signed statement from* *the RMO. The Vendor recommends sending a 15-day Non-Compliance letter and drafting an MTF explaining and providing emails documenting their attempts to obtain the signed affidavit.*

Action/Reaction: *The Investigator informs the Vendor with whom they contract that they have not received documents. The Vendor has a different relationship with the Agency than the Investigator and the documents are provided for the record shortly after the Vendor follows up.*

Action/Reaction: *The Investigator informs the Vendor with whom they contract that they are waiting for a statement from a key decision maker. The Vendor advises them to find out how much time the witness needs and to see if the CP would be willing to extend the investigative period to provide ample time to obtain testimony.*

Let's flip things around. We will go over some examples of when the Investigator is not patient or makes poor choices to address delays.

Action/Reaction: *The Investigator sends multiple emails to the CP, a demand letter, contacts their supervisor, and leaves urgent voice messages. The EEO Director sends an email with multiple people copied relaying that the CP is in the hospital and is not in the condition to work on their EEO complaint. How would the Investigator feel then?*

Action/Reaction: *Since the Investigator is unable to obtain the signed statement from an RMO, they contact the RMO's Supervisor, and the Investigator contacts the EEO Specialist who is their POC. The RMO cuts communication with the Investigator since they "threw them under the bus." The EEO Specialist provides advice on how* *the Investigator should proceed but thinks, "Why do I have to tell the Investigator how to do their job?"*

Action/Reaction: *Since the Investigator has not received documents from their Agency POC, they contact the POC's Supervisor who is the EEO Manager. The Vendor receives a call from the EEO Manager stating that the Investigators should not contact her. The EEO Specialist will always remember that Investigator because they "threw them under the bus" to their supervisor. The relationship between the Investigator and the POC will be strained going forward.*

Action/Reaction: *The key decision maker who is no longer a federal employee is not providing a statement in a timely fashion, so the Investigator sends multiple emails, leaves voicemails, and repeats the process. The decision maker is retired and decides they no longer want to participate because they are being pushed. They also send an email to some of the higher-up contacts at the Agency with whom they are still close. How will that email characterize the Investigator?*

Escalation is the key sometimes, however, if Investigators escalate too soon or to the wrong person they could be "stepping on someone's toes" or being the "annoying fly at a picnic."

Key points: There are protocols in place for situations like these. It is important to respect the chain of command. Investigators should notify their Vendors to escalate matters.

However, even when the Investigator makes the right choices, matters can still be delayed, and frustration is inevitable. Prudence is essential; always follow protocol and do not let impatience result in bad decisions and permanent damage to relationships.

Questions:

Unfortunately, there are not required trainings that would allow Investigators to work on drafting interrogatories. In addition to discrimination laws, there are specific areas that Investigators must grasp, such as progressive discipline and other applicable employment policies and laws, in order to be successful.

Example: An employee alleges they are being discriminated against based on a protected class (race) when they were suspended for five days without pay.

Seasoned Investigators understand that some employment actions cannot be taken against employees or approved without certain prerequisites. (1) Documentation, (2) Guidance from Human Resources, and (3) Observation of the Chain of Command, are some specific requirements for a serious employment action in the circumstance above. We will go over these three prerequisites and some of the questions the Investigator may ask to extract information about the 5-day suspension without pay.

#1: Documentation: Before a serious employment action is warranted there must be documentation or proof of unprofessional behavior and/or actions to justify a recommended discipline. Below are some questions the Investigator can ask to extract relevant information on what documentation Management has obtained for the 5-day suspension.

Questions: What occurred leading up to the suspension of Complainant? Was Complainant ever warned or counseled about these action(s)/behavior(s)? Was the Complainant given a chance to improve these action(s)/behavior(s)? How long did these action(s)/behaviors(s) persist? Is there any evidence that can be provided to justify the proposed suspension?

It is important for the Investigator to identify the primary reason for the Complainant's suspension, and document if the behavior is continuous or a one-time occurrence.

#2: Guidance from Human Resources: Depending on the severity of the behavior and the proposed discipline, prior to deciding on an employment action, Management often consults with HR for guidance. Below are some questions the Investigator will ask Management.

Questions: With whom did you consult in HR regarding Complainant's 5-day suspension? What role did HR play in the 5-day suspension and what did they recommend?

The Investigator should attempt to identify what influence HR had on the outcome and the justification for the decision. Did they follow the Table of Penalties or consider the Douglas Factors to decide the length of the suspension? What specific policies or protocols were used for guidance?

#3: Chain of Command: The federal government uses a chain of command for reporting and making decisions. There are usually multiple people involved in an employment action when the employment action is serious. It is important for the Investigator to find out who specifically made which decision, whether it was a consensus, and what specifically influenced the outcome.

Questions: Who proposed the decision? Who made the final decision? On what was the final decision-based? How did Management/HR arrive at the determination of five days without pay? Was any other Management official directly involved in the decision to suspend the Complainant for five days without pay?

It is common practice that the first-level Supervisor recommends and makes the decision, and the second-level Supervisor concurs and signs off on the 5-day suspension.

Keynote: It is important that Investigators avoid asking compound questions which can result in unanswered testimony.

Concern: If the appropriate questions are not drafted, it will result in an insufficient investigation which would require supplemental testimony. Simply put, supplemental testimony consists of responses to questions that should have been asked from the start. It causes delays, remands, annoys respondents, and is a waste of everyone's time.

Drafting effective questions is an art form that can take years to perfect. The quality of the testimony received is usually based on the effectiveness of the questions. This tends to be the foundation of the investigation.

AES will provide the blueprint for drafting effective questions in Chapter 7 which will shorten the learning curve.

CHAPTER 6

Comparators

Comparators/Circumstantial Evidence

One of the most confusing and difficult topics to grasp is the identity of a true comparator, and understanding how they are relevant in an EEO Investigation. A significant percentage of Investigators struggle to understand this key piece of circumstantial evidence.

The ability to master this skill set is a differentiator among Investigators and separates the great ones from the pack. This chapter will be a deep dive into different scenarios and strategies and will explain how comparator information is beneficial and can be utilized to improve the quality of ROIs.

Additionally, references on comparators are in **Chapter 5** (how to find comparators), and **Chapter 7** (how to draft questions for comparators).

Let's go over a few facts about circumstantial evidence/comparators.

- Investigations are more likely to extract, identify, and accumulate circumstantial evidence than direct evidence. This makes comparators a key piece of evidence.
- Documented and properly presented circumstantial evidence is sufficient for a case file, compared to accumulating fluff testimony, gossip and hearsay, and non-related details.
- Investigators are expected to find or inquire about a similarly situated comparator(s) for every disparate treatment case; An element of the Prima Facie specifically notes this key point.
- By understanding the importance of comparators and comparative evidence/data, Investigators are equipped to address the required element of the Prima Facie for alleged disparate treatment.
- Not every case will have a comparator, but efforts must be made to identify them if they exist.

Keynote: In the case where no comparator is identified, it is helpful if the Investigator drafts a memorandum to the file stating why a comparator cannot be identified.

We are going to provide multiple scenarios below and address the way an Investigator can effectively extract accurate information on comparators for the case file.

Circumstance #1:

One witness stated that every woman at the facility made plenty of mistakes, some serious in nature, but the Complainant (male) was the only employee fired by Charlie (Supervisor) for making similar mistakes. Unfortunately for the Complainant, there is no evidence on Agency record for extensive mistakes made by the female employees at the facility or what discipline they received, if any.

The Investigator needs to identify a comparator for the example above. How can the Investigator extract the facts for the record that address the alleged disparate treatment between the Complainant and the co-workers at the facility?

Below is information that has been obtained by the Investigator through multiple interrogatories:

Information #1: Sharon (Witness) said the Supervisor Charlie loves having women around to flirt with, so they are never held accountable for their actions.

Information #2: Keisha (Witness) relays that Charlie does not like the Complainant; they have a personality conflict and Charlie "steps on his toes" whenever he gets a chance.

Information #3: Mr. Martin, Safety Supervisor (Witness) provided a letter explaining there are five employees in the same position and unit under Charlie's supervision that did not respond to the safety alarm, including Complainant. Complainant received a reprimand that went into his personal file; the other four employees who were female were provided with a verbal warning.

Information #4: Jessica (Witness) stated that Charlie should never have been a supervisor; he is always late to work and submits his performance evaluations for employees past the allocated timeframe.

The Investigator has identified four comparators based on evidence (Information #3) he received from the Safety

Supervisor, Mr. Martin. The comparators were four women in Complainant's unit, who did not respond to the safety alarm and were not disciplined.

Why was Complainant reprimanded but the four comparators were given a verbal warning?

Next, the Investigator will now need to find out why these comparators were treated differently in a similar situation.

The Investigator can now focus on asking the decision maker, Charlie (Supervisor) how and why he made his decision to reprimand the Complainant, and why he gave the other four employees, who were female, verbal warnings for the same employment infraction.

Circumstance #2:

Below are comments from Administrative Law Judges (AJs) regarding comparators after reading Reports of Investigations:

1. AJ found that rotations were stopped for everyone and that Complainant was not treated any differently than the other employees in the unit.
2. AJ found that the Complainant clarified that she was not denied overtime, but she alleged that when she worked overtime, other employees were not assigned to help her. However, AJ noted that Complainant had not shown that anyone else was provided help with their work while working overtime.
3. AJ found that Complainant was not singled out and that others were also asked to cover the front desk when the unit was short-staffed.

4. AJ found that Complainant did not show that the events referenced in the suspension did not occur; or that others behaved in a similar manner and were not disciplined.

It is imperative to uncover what other employees in the same environment are experiencing. Digging deeper to capture the scope/context and details of a situation may be necessary to identify if someone is **a true comparator**.

Based on the AJs' comments, it appears the Investigator did a thorough job in each example to obtain information for the record and illustrate the context of the circumstances with pertinent details.

The first AJ's comment shows the Investigator interviewed the decision maker to determine who was affected by the employment action (rotations). Everyone was treated the same; therefore, no comparator was identified.

The second AJ's comment shows the Investigator was unable to find anyone who was treated differently than her while working overtime. Therefore, no comparator was identified.

The third AJ's comment illustrates some sort of corroboration was added to the file by the Investigator, possibly interviewing similarly situated comparators in the work environment to see if they performed the same duties as Complainant. No comparator was identified.

The fourth AJ's comment shows that the Investigator was unable to find any comparators for the record that behaved in a similar manner to Complainant. There is no comparator for the record.

Although in all four circumstances, no comparators were identified, the AJs noted that the correct efforts were made by the Investigators to address circumstantial evidence in each situation. The details are beneficial, as the AJs were able to make a determination.

Circumstance #3:

RMO response: In response to Complainant's claim that overtime was disproportionately given to African Americans, the RMO (Ms. Red Horse) stated that only Mr. Washington (African American employee) had more overtime hours than Complainant, and that was because he chose to perform 15 ultrasounds on Saturdays, while Complainant declined. The Agency found that the record showed Complainant worked 217.63 hours of overtime in fiscal year 2023, while the African American employees worked 197.5 and 153.3 hours. Additionally, Complainant worked 252.7 overtime hours in fiscal year 2022, as compared to 136.5 and 227.5 overtime hours for the African American employees.

In the example above, the Investigator had to use different methods to identify a comparator and gather circumstantial information for the file. We will go over two strategies combined for this scenario: Specific Data Request and Targeted Testimony.

Data: Asking employees for overtime data will not result in accurate data for the record nor can the Investigator trust the data is not altered by the employee. The Investigator should ask the Agency for comparative evidence for the record by making a specific inquiry into overtime hours for employees in the same position. By doing this, the data will show whether there is a disparity in the overtime hours.

Example: **Specific data request:** Provide data for the periods of FY2021 – FY2023 on overtime hours worked for all GS-14 Physicians under the supervision of Ms. Red Horse, in the Labor Division. Annotate the data by name, position title, unit, grade, race, and total of overtime hours for each fiscal year.

Note: In the scenario provided, there appears to be a disparity in overtime hours; therefore, the Investigator would need to take additional steps to verify if employees noted in the data request are true comparators.

Targeted Testimony: When looking at the example above, simply requesting data on employees' overtime hours does not tell the full story of why there is a disparity in hours. The Investigator needs to craft targeted question(s) based on evidence obtained through the specific data request. The next step would be to interview the decision maker (Ms. Red Horse) and ask specific questions as to why there appears to be a disparity in overtime hours, how the decision(s) were made, and why.

Example: **Targeted Testimony:** Data shows that Complainant received 217.63 overtime hours and Mr. Washington received 333.33 overtime hours. Explain the reason for the difference in overtime between these two employees.

Note: Mr. Washington was the proposed comparator in this case, as he was in a similar situation as CP (same Supervisor/position title), had a different race, and had more overtime hours than CP.

Ms. Red Horse provided key information that addressed the disparity in overtime hours. CP declined to do ultrasounds on Saturdays, while Mr. Washington did ultrasounds and accumulated a large amount of overtime.

Identifying Mr. Washington as a comparator and obtaining additional information was beneficial in determining if the disparity is based on race, or possibly something else.

Circumstance #4:

Non-selection comparators/evidence: The different comparators for competitive selection

> **Note:** McDonnell Douglas teaches that it is the plaintiff's task to demonstrate that similarly situated employees were not treated equally. 411 U.S., at 804.s

Non-selection case: The applicant selected for the position to which the Complainant applied, who has a different protected class than Complainant, *could* be the comparator. To make sure applicants are similar in this situation, specific details must be extracted. Simply applying for the same position is not enough to consider applicants similar. To determine if applicants are similar, the Investigator should gather information on the vacancy criterion. The Investigator needs to compare applicants' credentials (education or experience), how they were interviewed, and/or feedback from references.

Scenario: The applicant selected (Selectee) for the vacant position and CP both had the same master's degree and years of experience in science cloning, scored equally on resumes and interview scoring, had excellent references, and were both referred to the Selecting Official for consideration. However, the only difference between the two applicants was their National Origin.

In the above scenario, the Investigator has identified a comparator that is similarly situated, someone who applied to the same position, is equally qualified and was selected.

The next step would be to ask the Selecting Official how they made their selection for the position, why the selectee was chosen over CP, and what specific information was considered in their decision.

Non-referral case: All applicants referred for an interview or consideration to the next level in the selection process that have a different protected class than Complainant, could be a possible comparator. This could be an extensive number of employees and the Investigator would need to obtain this data through a Document Request.

Example: **Document Request:** Provide a list of applicants referred for the position of Head Science Cloner, SES, under vacancy #SES-SC-00010020, annotated with each applicant's name, and [Insert applicable protected class].

This request will allow the Investigator to see all potential comparators.

The next step would be to view the list of applicants and highlight those that have a different protected class than CP. Those applicants that are highlighted are comparators.

The Investigator now needs to identify the person responsible for not referring the CP. Questions should be asked on how that person made this decision to refer individuals, what specific rating system was used, and why Comparators were referred, but CP was not.

Not qualified: All applicants that made the certificate of eligibility and have a different protected class than Complainant could be a comparator. This could be an extensive list, consisting of a few to hundreds of applicants. The Investigator should obtain a list of the certificate of eligibles, annotated with the applicable protected class(es).

Example: **Document Request:** Provide the certificate of eligibility for the position of Head Science Cloner, SES, under vacancy #SES-SC-00010020, annotated with each applicant's name, and [Insert applicable protected class].

The investigative inquiry for this type of non-selection claim will focus on Human Resources or the division that assesses applicant packages.

Note: More than likely, the HR professional responsible for the decision at this stage in the application process is not aware of any of the applicants' names or specifics of their employment packages.

The Investigator will ask the HR official(s) how they made the decision to qualify applicants, what criterion was considered in their decision, why CP did not make the certificate of eligibles list, if they were aware of CPs protected class(es), and if that protected class(es) was noted somewhere in the employment package.

Circumstance #5:

Harassment/Hostile Work Environment (HWE):

Harassment is one of the most common types of discrimination complaints.

Note: Harassment/Hostile Work Environment (HWE) is subjective and personal; therefore, the Investigator needs to pay attention to the context and full scope of what is being alleged so they can ask questions to others who may have experienced similar actions or behaviors, but in a different way, in the same environment.

The Harassment Prima Facie does not have an element that requires a comparator. Some Agencies do not require a comparator to be identified, while others want to know who was treated differently in the same environment. We will show you how to extract circumstantial evidence for a hostile work environment claim. Below is an example of a harassment case.

Appellate decision scenario: "The Agency found that many of the instances of alleged harassment were related to Complainant's requests for overtime, her job duties, and workplace conditions, which also applied to the other employees who held the same position."

Based on the information in the example above, it appears the Investigator interviewed others in the work environment so the AJ could determine if their situation differed from the Complainant's when related to overtime, job duties, and workplace conditions.

Let's investigate how the Investigator attempted to find comparators.

In the situation of an HWE, the Investigator can simply look at the Workforce Profile or Organizational Chart to determine who is similarly situated (share a work environment) to the Complainant. A potential comparator could be anyone who shares the same work environment or position with the alleged harasser.

Keynote: In an HWE case, the specific allegations of harassment must be examined to determine accurate comparators. For this example, that would be overtime, job duties, and workplace conditions.

The work environment could contain many employees; therefore, the Investigator should ask the Complainant a series of questions to obtain potential comparators.

Sample Question: Was there anyone in your work environment who **was not** harassed or subjected to a hostile work environment in reference to overtime, job duties, or workplace conditions? If so, provide their names, division, unit, position title, grade, and [Insert protected class]

Sample Question: Was there anyone in your work environment who **was also** harassed or subjected to a hostile work environment in reference to overtime, job duties, or workplace conditions? If so, provide their names, division, unit, position title, grade, and [Insert protected class].

Notice how we are trying to request information on those not allegedly harassed, and those allegedly harassed. For a harassment case, this is a useful method to uncover additional circumstantial evidence.

For a harassment case, potential comparators are usually identified as "witnesses" since they are in the same environment. It is usually not necessary to interview comparators, but with harassment claims, it is necessary.

Next, the Investigator needs to obtain testimony from employees in the same work environment and document their experiences.

When information is obtained through testimony of employees in the alleged HWE, the following matrix can be drafted to clearly illustrate responses for the record.

Employee name	Sex	Age	Race	Claims HWE
Greg	Male	45	Asian-Pacific	Yes
Erin	Female	68	Black	No
Anthony	Male	43	Caucasian	No
Cynthia	Female	47	Caucasian	No
Complainant	Female	41	Asian	Yes

In addition to interviewing employees in the work environment, the Investigator can expand their request to obtain circumstantial information by analyzing recorded harassment complaints made against the alleged RMO in the case.

***Example*: Document Request:**

Provide two years of harassment claims (FY2021 - FY2023) filed against the RMO, annotated by the Complainant's name, position title, sex, age, race, and reason for the complaint.

Drafting comparator questions:

Many Investigators have a habit of drafting the questions to say: **Can you provide anyone who was treated more favorably than you under similar circumstances?**

Depending on with whom the Investigator is speaking, some people will not understand the question above. Other EEO Investigators, EEO Specialists, or Labor Law Attorneys will understand this question. However, Investigators are drafting questions for the Complainant, RMOs, and witnesses who do not have extensive EEO knowledge.

> **Note:** Drafting detailed comparator questions is especially important if the CP does not have representation.

Investigators with experience will inquire: Who are you comparing yourself to who was not discriminated against based on age?

As noted above, drafting questions that spell out the requirements for being similarly situated are necessary because a respondent may need more details to provide a complete response. Investigators should ask for specific information and note the employment action they are inquiring about; See below.

Seasoned Investigators will ask the following questions: To whom are you comparing yourself? Who has the same position and Supervisor as you, and missed the same meeting, but was not reprimanded? Identify them by name, position title, division/unit, Supervisor, and age.

After the Investigator obtains testimony and a comparator from the CP, the next step is to draft a question for the RMO. A seasoned Investigator will draft a custom question with specific details from CP's testimony; See below:

Example: **Question:** CP states that on January 23, 2023, like the Complainant, Joey Brown also skipped the meeting **(behavior/ action)** but was not reprimanded **(employment action)**. Is that true? Why was CP reprimanded and not Joey Brown when both missed the meeting? **(Similar circumstances)**.

> **Note:** In bold is key information that should be addressed when drafting a thorough question. It is shown as an example and is not to be included as part of the question.

Below is a comparator exercise for a professional to hone one of the most difficult EEO skills to master.

Comparator Exercise

Margaret Brown is a Black female who applied for a position and was not selected. The person selected for the position was a white Male in his 30s.

(Q) Who is the comparator? (Q) How many comparators are there? (Q) Who would be in a similar situation? (Q) Is more information necessary to find a comparator?

Michael Smith is a 65-year-old male who received a "Minimally Satisfactory" review on his Performance Management Appraisal Plan (PMAP). Other employees in the same division but different units that are 40 years old and younger received "Satisfactory" ratings on their PMAPs.

(Q) Who is the comparator? (Q) How many comparators are there? (Q) Who would be in a similar situation? (Q) Is more information necessary to find a comparator?

Jessica Johnson is a light tan-skinned African American female who was not promoted to the next GS grade. Another employee, a dark-skinned African American female, under the same Supervisor, received a promotion for two consecutive years.

(Q) Who is the comparator? (Q) How many comparators are there? (Q) Who would be in a similar situation? (Q) Is more information necessary to find a comparator?

In October 2013, Julia Russ (Complainant) (white female), found out that she would be promoted to the next GS grade. In January 2014, Ms. Russ found out from the HR Specialist that other male employees that have been promoted to the same GS grade as she but had received a 7% increase in their salary while she only received a 3% cost of living raise.

(Q) Who is the comparator? (Q) How many comparators are there? (Q) Who would be in a similar situation? (Q) Is more information necessary to find a comparator?

Abioye Mustaf (African, male) was charged 5.5 hours of Absence Without Leave (AWOL).

(Q) Who is the comparator? (Q) How many comparators are there? (Q) Who would be in a similar situation? (Q) Is more information necessary to find a comparator?

Argentina Cole, (Disability: physical and mental) has requested that her supervisor grant her three days of Telework because she gets depressed has panic attacks, and cannot drive during these attacks. The Supervisor denied Complainant's request for telework.

(Q) Who is the comparator? (Q) How many comparators are there? (Q) Who would be in a similar situation? (Q) Is more information necessary to find a comparator?

Additionally, when Ms. Cole's telework request was denied, she filed an EEO discrimination case against the Management officials (RMOs). After the RMOs found out that Ms. Cole (Complainant), had initiated an EEO case of discrimination against them, they subsequently assigned Ms. Cole duties that she is not qualified to perform and for which she has no training.

(Q) Who is the comparator? (Q) How many comparators are there? (Q) Who would be in a similar situation? (Q) Is more information necessary to find a comparator?

Mr. Greg Levy (disabled veteran) has requested that his immediate Supervisor grant him five days a week of telework. His immediate Supervisor has allowed other disabled veterans to telework for five days a week.

(Q) Who is the comparator? (Q) How many comparators are there? (Q) Who would be in a similar situation? (Q) Is more information necessary to find a comparator?

Kristina Kim (female, Asian, weak heart) is an International Travel Sales Executive. In March 2014, the Complainant received a note from the doctor stating that, due to her health, she should not be traveling long hours, and this note was included in her personnel file. The Complainant's Supervisor read the doctor's note in her personnel file and denied her promotion months later stating that she did not meet the basic requirements for the promotion.

(Q) Who is the comparator? (Q) How many comparators are there? (Q) Who would be in a similar situation? (Q) Is more information necessary to find a comparator?

Dr. Robert Monk (male, Caucasian) overheard his co-worker making derogatory comments about same-sex marriage, "gays," and making references to the Bible. The co-worker who was making the comment was aware that Mr. Monk, the Complainant, has been married to his same-sex partner for 10 years, and this is not the first time his co-worker has made these types of comments.

(Q) Who is the comparator? (Q) How many comparators are there? (Q) Who would be in a similar situation? (Q) Is more information necessary to find a comparator?

Additionally, after Mr. Monk had complained to his supervisor about his co-worker, Mr. John Klein, regarding the derogatory comments, Management had requested Mr. Klein to attend LGBT training and sexual discrimination training. Mr. Klein (male, Catholic) has raised a complaint against the Management officials for allegedly forcing him to attend meetings that are against his religious beliefs.

(Q) Who is the comparator? (Q) How many comparators are there? (Q) Who would be in a similar situation? (Q) Is more information necessary to find a comparator?

Ms. Donna Port (Female, late 20s, Spain) was hired for an assistant position within the Agency. Mr. Damian Croks, (male, late 40s, France) the Complainant's direct Supervisor, always comments on the Complainant's shoes, sends her flowers anonymously, and brings her chocolate-shaped hearts. When the Complainant refuses Mr. Croks' actions, he subsequently assigns her additional assignments and threatens her with disciplinary action and termination of her employment.

(Q) Who is the comparator? (Q) How many comparators are there? (Q) Who would be in a similar situation? (Q) Is more information necessary to find a comparator?

Understanding who is a viable comparator, how to identify them, and how to properly draft a question to find them will improve the quality of the Investigation. The Investigation will be superior and suitable for use at higher levels in the process.

The next chapter is going to provide step-by-step instructions on how to draft questions for the Investigative Plan. This is exciting as there is no comprehensive resource on how to do this and Investigators are usually "thrown to the wolves."

CHAPTER 7

Drafting Questions "The Blueprint"

The industry has a saying that there is no blueprint for investigating EEO matters. However, there is a blueprint for successfully drafting questions!

AES has shown in the previous chapters that using practical investigative skills is beneficial. Instructional Templates will complement practical skills and EEO knowledge guiding professionals to produce a sufficient work product.

This chapter is beneficial as it illustrates how to effectively draft questions. Below is a template (tool) on how to create relevant questions for an investigation by using the applicable Prima Facie.

LET'S GET STARTED...

A. Start with the accepted issue.

> **On January 1, 2018, the Complainant alleges he was discriminated against based on his race when he received a proposed 3-day suspension letter from his first-level Supervisor (James Smith).**

B. Next, determine the type of discrimination(s) and the Prima Facie: See below.

Prima Facie Case: In order to establish a prima facie case of disparate treatment, the Complainant has the burden of proof and must present evidence that:

(1) **He/she/they** belong(s) to a protected class because of **his/her/their** [Insert protected class].
(2) **He/she/they** was/were subjected to an adverse employment action; and
(3) There was a connection between membership in the protected class and the adverse employment action.

Management's Burden: Once Complainant establishes a prima facie case, the Agency must:

(1) Articulate a legitimate, non-discriminatory reason for the action taken.

Rebuttal: The Complainant retains the ultimate burden of proof to show that:

Management's articulated reason is pretext to hide discrimination.

CREATING THE QUESTIONS FOR THIS ACCEPTED INCIDENT

Below are standard preliminary questions used for every case:

1. For the record, state your name.
2. What is your current position title, grade, and agency unit/division?
3. How long have you been in this position? How long with this agency?
4. Who are your first-level and second-level Supervisors, by name and position title?

5. What is your working relationship with [Insert involved employees]? (The investigator can find this information in the counseling report).
6. State for the record your [Insert relevant protected class]. (For this example, the relevant protected class is race).

After the preliminary questions insert accepted issue verbatim:

On January 1, 2018, the Complainant alleges he was discriminated against based on his race when he received a proposed 3-day suspension letter from his first-level Supervisor (James Smith).

USING THE PRIMA FACIE TO MAKE QUESTIONS

Full Purview: The Investigator's purview is to cover the accepted issue and directly-related information only, to include supporting evidence/details and background information that addresses the alleged adverse action, and to cover the nexus (relation between protected class and adverse action).

Use the relevant Prima Facie to create the list of questions that must be addressed.

The first element of the Prima Facie: "He/she/they belong(s) to a protected class because of his/her/their [Insert protected class]."

This is addressed in question **# 6** above for standard questions. Below is the final question.

Q: "State for the record your race."

The second element of the Prima Facie: "He/she/they was/were subjected to an adverse employment action."

The adverse action is the focal point of the Investigator's purview. In this case, the adverse action is a **proposed 3-day suspension,** so questions will be made to verify and address this matter in detail.

Helpful Hint: The Investigator needs to extract background information on this adverse action (proposed 3-day suspension). This is where the Investigator should utilize the **who, what, when, where, why, and how** questions to create inquiries that will gather info to illustrate the background and foundation of this adverse action.

Q: Who issued you the proposed 3-day suspension, when and how? Provide their name, position title, and race (if known). (If you request identification for anyone during the investigation, always obtain the relevant protected classes of the complaint. This could be a potential form of evidence.)

Note: When asking questions, you need background details for the case, so a reviewer can visualize the circumstances and have detailed information to assess/analyze the context of the situation.

Q: What was the reason provided for the proposed 3-day suspension?

Q: Why did the Agency make the decision to propose a 3-day suspension?

Note: Every action or directive in the government usually has a certain protocol or policy that should be followed. The Investigator needs to understand how this policy applies to the situation they are investigating and uncover if there are other factors involved.

Q: Is there an Agency policy and/or protocol in reference to proposed suspensions? If so, please explain your understanding of this policy/protocol.

Asking questions on policy will allow a reviewer to compare testimony to the actual policy on file for corroboration.

The third element of the Prima Facie: "There was a connection between membership in the protected class and the adverse employment action."

Q: Why do you believe your race was the reason for receiving a proposed 3-day suspension?

Below are the questions we created so far:

1. For the record, please state your name.
2. What is your current position title, grade, and agency unit/division?
3. How long have you been in this position? How long with this agency?
4. Who are your first-level and second-level Supervisors, by name and position title?
5. What is your working relationship with [Insert involved parties]?
6. Please state for the record your race.
7. Who issued you the proposed 3-day suspension, when, and how? Provide their name, position title, and race (if known).

8. What was the reason provided for the proposed 3-day suspension?
9. Why did the Agency make the decision to propose a 3-day suspension?
10. Is there an Agency policy and/or protocol in reference to proposed suspensions? If so, please explain your understanding of this policy/protocol.
11. Why do you believe your race was the reason for receiving a proposed 3-day suspension?

We will now work on examining direct, circumstantial, comparative, and statistical evidence. Attempt to extract this evidence through identifying witnesses and determining viable comparators.

The logical way to find a witness(es) is by focusing on the adverse action. The goal when drafting proper witness questions is finding out who was involved, determining if anyone saw anything, or if that person would/should have been privy to this adverse action (proposed 3-day suspension).

Helpful Hint: The federal government uses a chain of command system, therefore, identifying and understanding the Supervisory line of authority will extract information on who proposed, signed off, or made the final decision on an adverse action(s).

Q: Was anyone else involved in the proposed 3-day suspension besides your Supervisor (James Smith)? If so, what was their involvement and how were you made aware?

Q: Do you propose any witnesses that have evidence on why your race is the reason for the proposed 3-day suspension?

Key: See how one question asks for the involved parties so the Investigator can obtain people who should have been privy to the employment action taken. The other question asks specifically for someone who would have evidence of racial discrimination in relation to the employment action.

Comparator: A similarly situated individual with a different protected class from Complainant, who received a different outcome under similar circumstances, under the same Management chain. **Finding a comparator(s) is an effective method to examine circumstantial evidence.**

Key: Investigators should ask if there is anyone who **did not** receive a proposed 3-day suspension, **is not** of the same race as the Complainant, has the **same Management chain,** and did something that **should have resulted** in a similar disciplinary action(s). In general, you are looking for any disparate treatment, which is the relevant Prima Facie for this accepted issue.

Q: Was there anyone under the same Management chain who did not receive a proposed 3-day suspension for similar action(s)/behavior as yours? If so, what is their position title, race, and what action(s)/behavior did they allegedly exhibit?

Below are the questions we have so far:

1. For the record, please state your name.
2. What is your current position title, grade, and agency unit/division?
3. How long have you been in this position? How long with this Agency?

4. Who are your first-level and second-level Supervisors, by name and position title?

5. What is your working relationship with [Insert involved parties]?

6. Please state for the record your [Insert protected class].

7. Who issued you the proposed 3-day suspension, when, and how? Provide their name, position title, and race (if known).

8. What was the reason provided for the proposed 3-day suspension?

9. Why did the Agency make the decision to propose a 3-day suspension?

10. Is there an Agency policy and/or protocol in reference to proposed suspensions? If so, please explain your understanding of this policy/protocol.

11. Why do you believe your race was the reason for receiving a proposed 3-day suspension?

12. Was anyone else involved in the proposed 3-day suspension besides your Supervisor (James Smith)? If so, what was their involvement and how were you made aware?

13. Do you propose any witnesses that have evidence on why your race is the reason for the proposed 3-day suspension? (Asking for witnesses to discrimination and the Complainant's opinion on discrimination are two completely different purviews).

14. Was there anyone under the same Management chain who did not receive a proposed 3-day suspension that should have? If so, what is their position title, race, and what action(s)/behavior did they allegedly exhibit?

Note: The 14 questions drafted so far cover the applicable Prima Facie and are good foundation questions; next, we are going to examine supplemental questions that will thoroughly cover the Investigator's purview for an investigation.

In blue font below are supplemental questions that need to be added to the foundation questions.

1. For the record, please state your name.
2. What is your current position title, grade, and agency unit/division?
3. How long have you been in this position? How long with this Agency?
4. Who are your first-level and second-level Supervisors, by name and position title?
5. What is your working relationship with James Smith?
6. Please state for the record your race.
7. Was James Smith aware of your race? If so, when and how did he become aware?
8. Who issued you the proposed 3-day suspension, when, and how? Provide their name, position title, and race (if known).
9. What was the reason provided for the proposed 3-day suspension? Is the reason provided true? Please explain.
10. Why did the Agency make the decision to propose a 3-day suspension? How were you made aware?
11. Is there an Agency policy and/or protocol in reference to proposed suspensions? If so, please explain your understanding of this policy/protocol.
12. Was this policy and/or protocol followed for the proposed 3-day suspension? If not, please explain.

13. Were you warned and/or counseled prior to being issued the proposed 3-day suspension? If so, when, how, and by whom?

14. Why do you believe your race was the reason for receiving a proposed 3-day suspension?

15. Was anyone else involved in the proposed 3-day suspension besides your Supervisor (James Smith)? If so, what was their involvement and how were you made aware?

16. Do you know who recommended and who made the final decision on the proposed 3-day suspension? If so, please state their name, position title, and race. (Complainants will not always know everyone who was involved at the management level, but it needs to be understood who they feel is discriminating against them based on their protected class).

17. Do you propose any witnesses for why your race is the reason for the proposed 3-day suspension?

18. Was there anyone under the same Management chain who did not receive a proposed 3-day suspension that should have? If so, what is their position title, race, and what action(s)/behavior did they allegedly exhibit?

19. Did you attempt to appeal the decision? If so, when and to whom? Who made the decision to uphold the 3-day suspension?

20. Is there anything else you would like to add that is relevant to the accepted issue(s) that has not already been covered?

21. Do you have any other witnesses that may have relevant information? If so, please describe to what they can attest. (Do not waste time interviewing witnesses that may not be relevant. Ask what they can attest to and make

a decision as to if they have relevant information or can corroborate other testimony).

22. What remedy do you propose?

Note: Questions 20, 21, and 22 are standard questions for all cases to close out the questioning.

RMO Questions

The prong of the applicable Prima Facie now moves to Management.

Management's Burden: "Once Complainant establishes a prima facie case, the Agency must articulate a legitimate, nondiscriminatory reason for the action taken."

Note: Investigators want to determine Management's **involvement**. Questions will be geared towards actions taken and the reasons why, if applicable.

Below, we are going to go over a few variables that an Investigator needs to address to extract relevant information pertaining to Management's involvement.

Chain of Command:

The federal government works in a chain of command much like the military. For certain employment actions to be approved, many Supervisors need approval from their Supervisors in the Management chain. (Sample **Q.:** What was your direct involvement in Complainant's 3-day proposed suspension, if any? If none, who was involved? Provide their name and position title.

Q.: Who recommended, and who made the final decision on the 3-day proposed suspension?)

Communication:

Investigators want to extract all communications the Management official(s) had with the Complainant based on the accepted issue. (Sample: **Q.:** Did you ever send the Complainant any emails or verbally relay anything to him about his proposed suspension?)

Precautionary measures:

Prior to a management official issuing a discipline or some type of adverse/tangible employment action they will usually issue a warning in the form of a memorandum (physical) or counseling (verbal); policies will usually outline the procedures for such employment directives. (Sample: **Q.:** Was the Complainant given any warning or counseling prior to receiving his proposed suspension?)

Nexus question: Make sure Management is on the record in the form of an affidavit to address that they did or did not discriminate against the Complainant based on his/her protected class. (Sample: **Q.:** Did Complainant's [Insert protected class] have any factor in your decision to issue his proposed suspension?)

Note: Do not accuse or assume that a management official did something; you will appear biased. Format the question so that you are asking them. Here is an example of the wrong way to frame a question. (Sample **Q.:** Why did you reprimand the Complainant? The Complainant said you were racist and made a racist slur; why did you do that?) **The**

correct way: (Sample **Q.:** The Complainant alleges that you are racist and made a racist slur in front of his co-workers. What is your response?)

Policy:

If the RMO cannot answer a policy question(s) or their testimony differs from the Complainant's concerning protocol or policy, the Investigator may need to ask a Human Resource Specialist or someone higher in the chain of command for information. (Sample: **Q.:** What is the relevant policy for a proposed suspension?)

Allegations:

In a typical investigation the Investigator will speak with the Complainant before they interview the responding Management officials. The Complainant will make allegations; if these statements are relevant to the accepted issue, the Investigator should present those allegations to Management for a response. (Sample: **Q.:** The Complainant alleges that you never provided him with safety instructions and blamed him for all major safety violations. Is that true? Please explain.)

Directions: Below are the questions verbatim from the Complainant's section above. In blue font below are the changes/adjustments the Investigator will need to make for the RMO questions.

1. For the record, please state your name.
2. What is your current position title, grade, and agency unit/ division?

3. How long have you been in this position? How long with this agency?

4. Who are your first-level and second-level Supervisors, by name and position title?

5. What is your working relationship with Complainant?

6. Please state for the record your race.

7. Were you aware of Complainant's race? If so, when and how did you become aware?

8. Who issued Complainant the proposed 3-day suspension, when, and how? Provide their name, position title, and race (if known).

9. What was your direct involvement in Complainant's 3-day suspension, if any? If none, who was involved? Provide their name and position title.

10. What was the reason provided for the proposed 3-day suspension? Was this relayed to the Complainant? If so, when and what was their response?

11. Is there an Agency policy and/or protocol in reference to proposed suspensions? If so, please explain your understanding of this policy/protocol.

12. Was this policy and/or protocol followed for the proposed 3-day suspension? If not, please explain.

13. Was Complainant warned and/or counseled prior to being issued the proposed 3-day suspension? If so, when, how, and by whom?

14. Do you know who recommended and who made the final decision on the proposed 3-day suspension? If so, please state their name, position title, and race.

15. Complainant alleges race is the reason for the proposed 3-day suspension. What is your response?

16. Was anyone else involved in the proposed 3-day suspension? If so, provide their name, position title, and explain their involvement.
17. Complainant states that employee X was not issued a suspension when participating in similar actions. Is that true? If not, what is your recollection of this?
18. Is there anything else you would like to add that is relevant to the accepted issue(s) that has not already been covered?
19. Do you have any other witnesses that may have relevant information? If so, please describe to what they can attest.
20. What remedy do you propose?

The questions above are a great foundation for the Investigative Plan.

The blueprint we provided shows that CP and RMO questions are similar as they are both focused on the theory of discrimination and relevant employment action. This is a neutral stance of questioning. The wording of the questions is adjusted to properly address the respondent and their involvement in the circumstances.

Each discrimination case is unique and may require additional or more thorough questions based on circumstances (parties involved, employee rank, employment status, background information).

Investigators now have a detailed example and useful tools for drafting preliminary questions that will help them successfully obtain the facts they need for a discrimination case.

CHAPTER 8

Drafting the Document Request (DR)

What is the purpose of the **Document Request**? A Document Request provided to the Agency is an attempt to obtain supportive and pertinent documents as background information and evidence for the accepted issues in the complaint.

One of the primary duties of an Investigator is to gather facts for the record.

The Investigator's purview involves obtaining the following types of evidence for the record: direct, circumstantial, comparative, and statistical.

There are different ways to gather evidence. Evidence will be gathered from the Complainant, witnesses, and other sources, such as the Agency through a Document Request.

To support findings and, ultimately, decisions, this evidence should be material to the complaint, relevant to the issue(s) raised in the complaint, and as reliable as possible. The three most **common** types of evidence obtained for the record are circumstantial.

Circumstantial Evidence: This is the evidence based on inference, in other words, the fact finder must draw an inference from the evidence to reach a factual conclusion.

Example: Complainant was not selected for the zookeeper position and believes his race (Latino) is the reason. The record shows that no Latino employees have been selected for a position in the last 15 years, which includes over 177 Latino applicants.

Comparative Evidence: This is circumstantial evidence based on how similarly situated persons outside of the Complainant's protected groups were treated.

Example: Five applicants were chosen for the zookeeper position; all five were Caucasian.

Statistical Evidence: This is circumstantial evidence provided through data that may show a disparity in treatment among employees.

Example: The record shows that of applicants selected over the last 15 years, 98% were white, 1% were Asian, and 1% were Native American.

Below AES will provide detailed step-by-step instructions on how to draft a Document Request. We will go over the standard documents that should be requested for the accepted incident.

Let's Get Started...

Background Information: The Complainant is Mr. Tim Tran, (race: Caucasian, sex: Male). His position title is an Immunization Technician, GS-6; he works for the Department of Infectious Diseases (DHD); Centers for Biological Warfare Control and Prevention (CBWC); World Commission (WC), Rockville, MD

Accepted Issue: On April 23, 2018, you were discriminated against based on race (Caucasian) and sex (Male) when Mr. Mitchel Smith, your "Direct Line Supervisor" switched your duties from "Project Manager GS-15/10 to a "GS-6 Tech" and had you doing manual labor.

Document Request: [Insert case number]

TO: [Insert Point of Contact's name and position title]
          [Insert POC's email address]

FROM: [Investigator's first and last name], Contract EEO Investigator
          [Insert contact information]

DATE: MM/DD/YYYY

RE: [Insert Complainant's first and last name and case number]
          Document Due Date – [Calculate 10-15 days from submittal of the Document Request]

I have been assigned to investigate the aforementioned formal EEO complaint. The following documents are essential for inclusion in the Report of Investigation. Please respond to this request by providing the documents **(one-sided copies only),** <u>organized, identified, and separated in the order as requested</u>. If the requested documents are voluminous, only relevant excerpts of the documents should be provided. Steps should be taken to avoid producing duplicate documents and email strings. A statement should accompany the documents from an appropriate official certifying the documents are true and accurate. **The statement should also include an explanation for any documents not produced.** Statements should be on official stationery, dated, and signed, and must include the title of the certifying official.

Since investigations are conducted under a strict statutory time frame, the timely return of the requested documents is needed. An adverse inference may be drawn by the adjudicator of the complaint if the Agency fails to provide the requested documentation. <u>Please forward the documents requested to me</u> **<u>no later than</u> [Insert the due date]** <u>to</u>:

> **Investigator's name,**
> **[Insert Investigator's email, phone]**

*Above is the **First page** which will contain basic case information and relevant contact information, which should all be provided in the Administrative File. This is an opportunity for the Investigator to address the due date for the record and address how they want the documents formatted and provided.

Note: It is imperative to tell the Agency how you want to receive the documents for efficiency and record-keeping purposes. Investigators will not want to deal with double-sided documents, and they should not make the due date a few days before they anticipate finishing the case as they will need ample time to review.

Note: It is imperative that Investigators double-check that they are using the correct names and case numbers. Many Investigators cut/paste information from one Document Request to another to save time but forget to change the case number.

*The **Second page*** will contain the relevant documents the Investigator is attempting to obtain which were not initially provided with the administrative case file.

Key tip: The best way for an Investigator not to miss any documents is to work on the Investigative Plan (IP) and Document (DR) simultaneously. As soon as they finish drafting the questions for the first Accepted Issue on the IP, they can then determine what documents they will need to effectively support that accepted issue, and then move on to drafting questions for the next issue.

Note: Many Investigators complete all their questions first, and then move on to drafting the DR but forget to request documents for some of the accepted issues.

DOCUMENT REQUESTS

The first two documents the Investigator will be requesting are the **Organizational Chart** and **Workforce Profile**.

Organizational Chart: This document delineates the chain of command. The Investigator must accurately verify that the Organizational Chart is for the correct Agency where the Complainant is employed. This document shows the chain of command and potentially allows the Investigator to identify other Management officials who may have been involved concerning some of the employment action(s) in the case.

Workforce Profile: This document is a list of employees located in a certain unit or division. It is important for the Investigator to narrow down a request to extract the pertinent information needed, e.g., employees' names, position titles, GS grade, and the employees' protected class(es) applicable to the specific case. By obtaining this information, the Investigator can potentially identify comparative data on employees in the Complainant's unit.

Note: The Investigator will get what they ask for so they should be careful to request information on employees that are under the same employment chain and unit/division and request that the profile is notated by the applicable protected class(es).

Note: For non-selection cases, Investigators must obtain the Organizational chart and Workforce Profile information for the Agency, Unit/Division and/or office for the position to which the Complainant applied.

Let's review, in detail the two documents requested so far:

1. **Organizational Chart for Department of Infectious Diseases (DHD); Centers for Biological Warfare Control and Prevention (CBWC); World Commission (WC), Rockville, MD to which Complainant reports as of April 23, 2018.**

2. **Workforce Profile for Department of Infectious Diseases (DHD); Centers for Biological Warfare Control and Prevention (CBWC); World Commission (WC), Rockville, MD to which Complainant reports as of April 23, 2018:**

   a. **Identify each employee by his/her organizational unit, name, position title, series, grade, race and sex, (if applicable).**

Note: Use the date associated with the accepted issue. If there are multiple issues in the case, then use the most recent date for the request.

The third request is for **Complainant's Position Description**. This is a standard request and will be asked for all cases. Notice that, in this example, we ask for two positions since the accepted issue addresses the Complainant being reassigned to another position. Request both so the duties can be compared if necessary.

3. **Copy of Complainant's Position Description for a Project Manager, GS-15/10, and Immunization Technician, GS-6, as of April 23, 2018.**

The fourth and fifth requests are for **any and all documents and email communications** for the adverse action(s) that are being investigated.

4. **Any and all documents and/or correspondence pertaining to Complainant's duties being changed from "Project Manager GS-15/10 to a "GS-6 Tech", dated, April 23, 2018.**

5. **Any and all documents and/or correspondence pertaining to Complainant having to do manual labor, dated April 23, 2018.**

Note: The Complainant may provide documents for the adverse action(s) voluntarily, but these documents may not be all-inclusive. The Investigator should also make the request to the Agency to obtain any other documents that may be relevant to the circumstances surrounding the issue(s). There may be some overlap and duplication, which is better than an incomplete file.

The sixth request is for the **SF-50** (Notification of Personnel Action Form) which is written documentation of a personnel action that affects an employee's position or pay. The **SF-52 Form** is used for supervisors and managers to request position action(s) such as the establishment of a new position or the reclassification of an existing position, or employee actions such as the appointment of an employee or a promotion. Note that SF-50s and SF-52s are not always relevant depending on the adverse action.

6. **SF-50 and SF-52s pertaining to Complainant's duties being changed, as of April 23, 2018, if applicable.**

The seventh request is for the Complainant's **Performance Evaluations**: These documents are required when the adverse action involves: demotion, performance evaluations, discipline actions, and other action(s) that may affect the duties or employment status of the Complainant. The Performance Evaluations are not always needed, but Investigators could consider them a standard document to request for 99% of cases.

7. **The Complainant's Performance Evaluations for Fiscal Year 2016-2018, including Mid-Year evaluations.**

The **eighth request** is for **Two-Year comparative data.** This information is requested to establish whether data exists for other employees experiencing the same adverse action(s) as the Complainant.

Note: It is important to list specific information (customized request), so the data results provided can be used for comparative analysis. See below for an example.

8. **Between the dates of April 23, 2016, and April 23, 2018, have any employees under Mr. Mitchel Smith's supervision had their duties changed from "Project Manager GS-15/10 to Immunization Technician, GS-6? If so, please state their name, title, and their race and sex, if known. What was the reason for the employment action?**

Note: The part about being assigned labor duties was omitted. Not everything will be recorded in Agency records. The Investigator should not take the chance of someone in the Agency responding that there are no records available because one part of the request does not match.

The **ninth request** is for **Agency Policies**: Each Agency and even different divisions within the same Agency may have different policies or excerpts so Investigators should make sure to <u>always</u> ask for the relevant policy in reference to the adverse action. Policies are large, so make sure you ask for specific excerpts of the policy to cover the case's adverse actions and unique circumstances. Once again, use the date from the accepted issue. If you have multiple issues, use the most recent date.

9. **Excerpts of relevant Agency policies, procedures, directives regarding: change in duties, demotions, assignment of labor duties, including relevant section(s) of the negotiated collective bargaining agreement, if applicable as of April 23, 2018.**

Below is the finished product for a Document Request based on the Accepted issue as an example:

Document Request: DHD-74848-2018

TO:	Ms. Melinda Crook, EEO Advisor MelindaCrook@DHD.gov
FROM:	Cindy Xaviar, Contract EEO Investigator 765-336-3837
DATE:	May 23, 2018
RE:	Mr. Tim Tran, CDC-74848-2018 Document Due Date – June 7, 2018

I have been assigned to investigate the aforementioned formal EEO complaint. The following documents are essential for inclusion in the Report of Investigation. Please respond to this request by providing the documents **(one-sided copies only)**, <u>organized, identified, and separated in the order requested</u>. If the requested documents are voluminous, only relevant excerpts of the documents should be provided. Steps should be taken to avoid producing duplicate documents and email strings. A statement should accompany the documents from an appropriate official certifying the documents are true and accurate. **The statement should also include an explanation for any documents not produced.** Statements should be on official stationery, dated, and signed, and must include the title of the certifying official.

Since investigations are conducted under a strict statutory time frame, the timely return of the requested documents is needed. An adverse inference may be drawn by the adjudicator of the complaint if the Agency fails to provide the requested documentation. <u>Please forward the documents requested to me</u> <u>**no later than June 7, 2018,**</u> to:

Cindy Xaviar
Cxaviar@advancedeeosolutions.com

DOCUMENT REQUESTS

1. Organizational Chart for Department of Infectious Diseases (DHD); Centers for Biological Warfare Control and Prevention (CBWC); World Commission (WC), Rockville, MD, to which Complainant reports as of April 23, 2018.

2. Workforce Profile for Department of Infectious Diseases (DHD); Centers for Biological Warfare Control and Prevention (CBWC); World Commission (WC), Rockville, MD to which Complainant reports as of April 23, 2018:

   a. Identify each employee by his/her organizational unit, name, position title, series, grade, race and sex, (if applicable).

3. Copy of Complainant's Position Description for a Project Manager, GS-15/10, and Immunization Technician, GS-6, as of April 23, 2018.

4. Any and all documents and/or correspondence pertaining to Complainant's duties being changed from "Project Manager GS-15/10 to a "GS-6 Tech" as of April 23, 2018.

5. Any and all documents and/or correspondence pertaining to Complainant's having to do manual labor, as of April 23, 2018.

6. SF-50 and SF-52s pertaining to Complainant's duties being changed, as of April 23, 2018.

7. The Complainant's Performance Evaluations for Fiscal Years 2016-2018, including Mid-Year evaluations.

8. Between the dates of April 23, 2016, and April 23, 2018, have any employees under Mr. Mitchel Smith's supervision had their duties changed from "Project Manager GS-15/10" to "Immunization Technician, GS-6," and been assigned labor duties? If so, please state their name, their title, their race, and sex, if known. What was the reason for the employment action?

9. Excerpts of relevant Agency policies, procedures, and/or directives regarding change in duties, demotions, assignment of labor duties, to include relevant section(s) of the negotiated collective bargaining agreement, if applicable as of April 23, 2018.

Other sources of documents:

Investigators will receive documents from the Agency and from affiants during the investigative stage. Affiants, especially the Complainant and RMOs, can be a great source of obtaining pertinent information. Make sure to put a footnote detailing who provided the information.

Receiving and sorting documents:

Most documents provided will be relevant to the case. Occasionally, there is what we call a "document dump" where the Agency sends a voluminous amount of information that needs to be sorted through to determine what is relevant. The Agency typically provides the specific documentation labeled according to what the Investigator requested.

If a voluminous number of documents is received from the Complainant, RMO and/or Witnesses, we recommend that the

Investigator ask for a Table of Contents (TOC) to clarify the identity of each document.

If the documents are unclear based on the subject matter, the Investigator should ask the sender to explain why or how it is relevant. When analyzing information provided, an Investigator should assess "How is this relevant to the Accepted Issues, supporting testimony, context, and background story provided?"

If the information provided is not relevant, the Investigator should draft an MTF explaining where they received the info, and why they are not including it in the record. The EEO Investigator has the responsibility and discretion to make the decision on what documentation is relevant for inclusion.

If any document is not legible, the Investigator should ask for a better version of the document. If a better version is not provided, then an MTF should be drafted to explain attempts to obtain a legible copy and email documentation should be included to support the MTF.

Duplicate Documentation:

It is common for the involved parties to provide the same documentation. If affiants provide a duplicate document(s) as an attachment behind their affidavit, it needs to be left "as is" because their testimony might refer to a specific attachment as a reference.

For documents not attached to or specifically referenced in affidavits, Investigators should remove duplicates of policies, SF-50/SF-52s, Performance Appraisals, Letters of Reprimand, and other employment directives.

Note: Email communications should always be left alone because a narrative could be altered by a sender providing bits and pieces of communication, and it could be extremely burdensome to determine the start or end of an email chain.

An important step of the investigative process is requesting, receiving, organizing, and labeling documents. Above, we have shown a step-by-step process on how to request the standard documents for an EEO complaint. Each case is unique, and Investigators can supplement their Document Request, as necessary.

The next Chapter will be an instructional template on how to draft an ROI.

CHAPTER 9

Drafting a Report of Investigation (ROI)

The ROI summarizes the investigative stage and documents the testimony and evidence obtained.

After preparing questions, interviewing affiants, collecting facts, and organizing evidence for the record, the Investigator will assemble an ROI as the last step in the investigative process.

This chapter will explain how an ROI should be drafted by assimilating case data to show where, why, and how it should be used. AES will address how to strategically summarize testimony to be thorough but concise, provide methods for EEO sufficiency, and break down statistical data.

Below is an ROI template to follow along. ROI templates will vary based on Agency preference, but the same information will be documented in every ROI.

DEPARTMENT OF [INSERT AGENCY]
REPORT OF INVESTIGATION

I. DESCRIPTION
OF COMPLAINT

Name of Complainant:

First & Last name
Stress Address
City, ST Zip

240-111-1111 (wk)
240-222-2222 (hm)
123-456-7890 (cell)

Case Number:

DHD-0000-2012

Complainant's Representative (if applicable):

N/A

Title and Grade of the Complainant's Position:

Lead Scientist, GS-14

Name and Location of Agency and Unit Involved:

Department of Infectious Diseases (DHD); Centers for Biological Warfare Control and Prevention (CBWC); World Commission (WC), Rockville, MD.

Date(s) of Alleged Discrimination:

December 20, 2012

Kind of Discrimination:

Retaliation/Reprisal (prior EEO activity, filed 9/6/2011)

Nature of Action, Decision, or Condition Giving Rise to Complaint:	Exclusion from meetings, Duties that do not align with Position Description (PD).

II. DESCRIPTION OF INVESTIGATION

Identity of Investigator:	[Insert Investigator's name] [Insert Subcontractor's name, LLC]
Place of Investigation:	Telephonic
Dates of Investigation:	December 2012 – March 2013

III. DESCRIPTION OF BASES AND ISSUES AND STANDARDS OF PROOF

[Insert issues verbatim from the acceptance letter.]

A. **Accepted Issue(s): Complainant alleges that he was discriminated against on the basis of reprisal/retaliation (prior EEO activity filed 9/6/2011), when he was subjected to the following incident:**

   1. **On December 20, 2012, he was excluded from an informative meeting and assigned duties that do not align with his position description (PD)**

[Insert the applicable Prima Facie below.]

B. **Theories**

   1. **Disparate Treatment: Reprisal**

Prima Facie Case: In order to establish a *prima facie* case of reprisal, Complainant has the burden of proof and must present evidence that:

1) Had Complainant previously engaged in protected activity or opposed unlawful discrimination?
2) Was the Agency aware of Complainant's activity?
3) Was Complainant contemporaneously or subsequently adversely affected by some action of the Agency?
4) Does some connection exist between Complainant's activity and the adverse employment decision (e.g., the adverse employment decision occurred within such a period of time that a retaliatory inference arises)?

OR

Is there direct evidence that shows discriminatory intent?

Rebuttal

What did the Agency say was the reason for the adverse employment decision?

Pretext

Is there direct or circumstantial evidence that the Agency's reason for the employment decision is pretextual?

IV. SUMMARY

> **Introduction Section:** This section introduces affiants that provided testimony and covers general background information. The standard questions asked for each case are summarized here as an introduction before addressing testimony associated with the accepted issue(s).

Affiants

Complainant, Dr. Jerome Talisker, (Prior EEO activity) is a *[Insert position title and GS-grade level]*, *[Insert Agency/Division/Unit/Office/Location]* Complainant has held this position for *[Insert number]* years and has been employed by the federal government for *[Insert number]* years. Complainant's first-level Supervisor is *[Insert first and last name]*, *[Insert position title]*. Complainant's second-level Supervisor is *[Insert first and last name]*, *[Insert position title]*. Complainant states that he filed an informal complaint on September 11, 2011. Complainant states that the RMOs were aware of his EEO complaint because they were involved. **(*Insert citation*)**

> **Note:** If someone has reprisal as a protected class, write a brief sentence explaining the action(s) to be considered covered by that protected class.

Responding Management Official (RMO), Dr. Ken Ardbeg, (Prior EEO activity) is the *[Insert position and GS-grade level]*, *[Insert Agency/Division/Unit/Office/Location]* He has held this position for *[Insert number]* years and has been with the Agency for/since *[Insert number] years*. His first-level Supervisor is

[Insert first and last name], *[Insert position title]*. His second-level Supervisor is *[Insert first and last name]*, *[Insert position title]*.

Below, we will cover additional information that should be covered for RMOs.

Tip: Mention the person's involvement in relation to the Complainant, i.e., Supervisor, co-worker, team lead, etc. *Example*: Dr. Ardbeg was Complainant's first-level Supervisor.

Tip: Mention the person's involvement in relation to the accepted issues, and mention what they did. *Example*: Dr. Ardbeg was alleged to have excluded Complainant from a meeting.

Tip: Mention if the RMO is aware of Complainant's protected class. *Example*: Mr. Ardbeg states he was involved as a Responding Management Official in one of Complainant's prior EEO complaints. (*Insert citation*) For prior EEO activity, it is important to summarize if and when the RMO was involved in CPs complaint or if and when they were aware.

See Dr. Laphroaig's section below for a comprehensive sample of what was addressed above.

Responding Management Official (RMO), Dr. Troy Laphroaig, (Prior EEO activity) is the *[Insert position and*

GS-grade level], in the [Insert Agency/Division/Unit/Office/ Location] He has held this position for [Insert number] years, and has been with the Agency for/since [Insert number] years. His first-level Supervisor is [Insert first and last name], [Insert position and GS-grade level]. His second-level Supervisor is [Insert first and last name], [Insert position title]. Dr. Laphroaig was the Complainant's Team Lead at the time of the alleged incident. He confirms that he was not involved in excluding the Complainant from a meeting. Dr. Laphroaig states that he was a witness in an EEO complaint that did not involve the Complainant. He learned of Complainant's EEO activity in this matter when he was contacted by the Investigator; *OR* He states that he is unaware of any prior EEO activity filed by Complainant. **(Exhibit 8)**

Complainant's Witness, Dr. Charles Bowmore, (No prior EEO activity) is the [Insert position and GS-grade level], in the [Insert Agency/Division/Unit/Office/Location] He has held this position for [Insert number] years and has been with the Agency for/since [insert number] years. His first-level Supervisor is [Insert first and last name], [Insert position title]. His second-level Supervisor is [Insert first and last name], [Insert position title]. [Mention the person's involvement in relation to the CP (such as: Supervisor, co-worker, team lead, etc.). **(Exhibit 9)**

Note: For witnesses, it is beneficial to point out the reason they were deposed

Tip: Mention their involvement or what they witnessed. *Example:* Dr. Bowmore contends that Complainant is treated unfairly in group meetings.

See below, Ms. Cairdeas' section for a comprehensive sample of what was addressed above.

Agency Witness/Subject Matter Expert (SME), Ms. Eileen Cairdeas, (No prior EEO activity), is the Human Resources Specialist, GS-12 in the DHD/... She has held this position for .... years, and has been with the Agency for/since... Her first-level Supervisor is *[Insert first and last name]*, *[Insert position title]*. Her second-level Supervisor is *[Insert first and last name]*, *[Insert position title]*. She states she has no working relationship with Complainant other than answering questions on Agency policies and employee rights. She confirms she advised the Complainant that he had a right to attend meetings which addressed responsibilities under his Position Description. She states that she was unaware the Complainant had prior EEO activity. **(Exhibit 10)**

Comparator, Dr. Eli Octomore, (No prior EEO activity), is a Lead Scientist, GS-13, in the Department of Infectious Diseases (DHD); Centers for Biological Warfare Control and Prevention (CBWC); World Commission (WC). He has held this position for... years, and has been with the Agency for/since... His first-level Supervisor is *[Insert first and last name]*, *[Insert position title]*. His second-level Supervisor is *[Insert first and last name]*, *[Insert position title]*. **(Exhibit 11)**

> **Note:** Comparators are only interviewed in certain situations.

> **Tip:** Mention this employee's experience in reference to the adverse action. ***Example:*** Dr. Octomore states that he has never been excluded from meetings.

Key Notes for Summary Section:

- The summary section should summarize testimony relevant to the accepted issue that is obtained during the interview process and should not read like an autobiography of the Complainant.
- Summaries should be thorough and concise; the Investigator should cover details pertaining to the accepted issues and any supplemental information that could possibly support those specific allegations.
- Sentences should be carefully written and grammatically correct, so it is clear who is speaking or acting.
- Investigators should read their summary a few times on different days so that they can notice any typos, grammatical errors, and/or gaps in testimony.

Complainant Summary Section

- In general, Investigators should summarize testimony relevant to the accepted issue and explain why Complainant believes the employment action was taken with regard to Complainant's protected class.
- Make sure sentences in the Complainant section start accordingly with the following:

  "The Complainant" or "Complainant states/asserts/ contends/opines/confirms, etc." Stay consistent on the use of "The Complainant" vs "Complainant." If the Investigator uses "Complainant," then they should use it throughout the ROI.

- Make an effort to summarize events that occurred in chronological order.

Below, we will walk through how to structure a summary in a way that effectively addresses the relevant prima facie case.

The relevant prima facie case is retaliation, **basis** (reprisal: prior EEO complaint), **adverse action**: Exclusion from meetings, and assignment of duties that do not align with Position Description.

Starting point: The summary of testimony should be organized by allegation.

Issues

1. **Issue: On December 20, 2012, he was excluded from an informative meeting and assigned duties that did not align with his Position Description (PD).**

First paragraph: Laying the Foundation

Information to be addressed includes but is not limited to the following: The Investigator should provide background information leading up to the alleged issue; The Investigator should not just "jump in" and state what happened without introducing the involved affiant(s) and their respective roles. They should briefly address Agency policy and procedures/protocols relevant to the accepted issue. In general, the Investigator should clarify who is responsible for what duties and establish who has authority over the situation.

Example: *Complainant states that his Position Description indicates that he should be responsible and oversee all duties in relation to creating, supervising, and controlling genetically modified diseases. The Complainant asserts that it is his duty to educate all scientists on new technology and compromised subject experiments during bi-weekly meetings.*

Note: In the first paragraph, the Investigator should prepare the reader for the issues that are about to be discussed. It makes an easier read if events flow in a chronological order throughout the summary paragraphs.

Second paragraph: Introducing the Adverse Action

Information to be addressed includes but is not limited to the following: This is the paragraph where the Investigator should address what happened. It is important to address the who, what, when, where, why, and how for all relevant circumstances, events, conversations, etc., related to the accepted issue. If it takes two paragraphs to explain this, that is fine, but Investigators should not go off on a tangent.

Example: *Complainant states that in 2012, his duties have slowly been replaced with duties that align with a Janitor's Position Description, such as cleaning hazardous material, dumping genetically modified excretions, and cleaning the incubator. Complainant states that he learned he was excluded from previous meetings pertaining to "new biological germs without cures" when he overheard other Scientists (names not disclosed) in the same office speaking in the hallway. The Complainant states that Dr. Laphroaig is responsible for scheduling all meetings and notifying participants of locations, dates, and times.*

> **Note:** This paragraph should illustrate all the players and their direct involvement according to the Complainant's testimony and/or perception of what occurred. Investigators should make sure to provide supplemental information that is relevant where necessary. ***Example***: *The Complainant states that all Scientists are required to sign confidentiality forms prior to attending each weekly meeting.*

Third paragraph: Introducing the Nexus

<u>Information to be addressed includes, but is not limited to the following</u>: How is the adverse action connected to the Complainant's protected class? This paragraph should mention comparators if any have been identified. Circumstantial and direct evidence (if obtained) should be used in this paragraph to document/illustrate alleged discrimination.

Example: *Complainant states he filed his prior EEO complaint against Dr. Ardbeg and Dr. Laphroaig in 2011. The Complainant states that he filed an EEO complaint against Dr. Ardbeg and Dr. Laphroaig because they accused him of being an "outsider" and fabricated lies against him about addressing unethical Agency procedures with a freelance journalist. Complainant states the exclusion from meetings and change in position duties (December 2012) happened subsequently after Complainant filed an EEO complaint against them for the incident. Complainant states that Dr.*

Eli Octomore (no prior EEO activity) is not excluded from meetings and handles all his regular duties as a Lead Scientist.

> **Note:** The Investigator should make sure that they are clear in defining when a previous complaint was filed and when the adverse action happened. This information is assessed by FAD writers for temporal proximity for reprisal claims, and a summary is helpful when the Investigator displays how much time elapsed.

RMO Summary Sections

- The first sentence of each paragraph should start with "Mr./Ms./Their Last name; thereafter, the Investigator should write "He/She/They states, contends, asserts, alleges that..." The main goal is to stay consistent and not flip-flop back and forth from writing the last name and then switching back and forth to he/she/they or the reader might become confused as to who is saying what.

- In general, summarize testimony relevant to the accepted issues, the Agency's defense for taking the employment action, and whether it was based on the Complainant's protected class.

- Corroborate testimony: Investigators should summarize affiant's specific involvement in an employment action to illustrate if they made a recommendation, final decision, concurred, or provided guidance.

First paragraph: Laying the Foundation

Information to be addressed includes but is not limited to the following: The paragraph should start with addressing the Agency policy relevant to the accepted issue, if applicable. Do not just jump in and state the RMO's actions had nothing to do with the Complainant's protected class. Explain in general who is responsible for what duties in the division/unit and who has authority.

Example: Dr. Ardbeg states that in 2011, the Complainant was identified and or discovered as being an "anonymous" Agency official in reference to an article written for an independent activist movement. Dr. Ardbeg states that discussing top secretive information with an outside source is against Agency policy according to a confidentiality agreement which must be signed by all active Scientists within DHD.

> **Note:** Keep in mind this is the RMO so their testimony will be heavier on the internal policy and procedures throughout most of their paragraphs. In the example above, the Investigator is documenting supplemental information that will be important when addressing Management's non-discriminatory reason later in the summary section.

Second paragraph: Addressing Management's Responsibilities

Information to be addressed includes, but is not limited to the following: This is the paragraph where the Investigator addresses who is responsible for the employment action relevant to the accepted issue. It is important to address who, what, when, where, why, and how for all relevant circumstances, events, conversations, etc., related to the accepted issue or other pertinent information disclosed during the investigation. It is important to make sure that one of the RMO summaries captures the decision maker(s)' actions and reasons. If an RMO testifies they were not involved, it is necessary to <u>find out who was.</u> If no one takes onus of an employment decision, the investigation is insufficient. Investigators should document attempts they made to obtain testimony from individuals who may have been involved in employment actions.

Example: *Dr. Laphroaig states that he oversees notifying employees of confidential meetings and making sure that their security clearance is up to date. Dr. Laphroaig alleges that Dr. Ardeg instructed him on February 2, 2012, that the Complainant was under internal investigation and advised him (Dr. Laphroaig) to take appropriate measures to ensure confidentiality and internal security protocols were met.*

<u>Third paragraph: Addressing Relevant Internal Procedures</u>

<u>Information to be addressed includes but is not limited to the following:</u> The Investigator should address the procedures, measurements, scales, directives, etc., for the employment issue at hand. This should be a technical paragraph that shows how all employees fall under the same review/Agency process. The process should be described in detail so that the reader understands what measures were taken and why regarding the employment action being investigated.

Example: *Dr. Ardbeg states that when an employee is under investigation, their duties default to "unclassified" according to HR Directive 12.DHD-5. Dr. Ardbeg states that all employees considered as unclassified are assigned duties at Management's discretion. Dr.*

Ardbeg states that depending on the allegations of charges/violation, an employee can be temporarily put on paid suspension, leave without pay (LWOP), or have their security clearance removed while an investigation is in progress.

> **Note:** It is important for the Investigators to illustrate or capture internal processes in reference to circumstances surrounding the Complainant's allegations. All involved participants and their direct involvement should be summarized.

Fourth paragraph: Addressing Nn-Discriminatory Reasons for Employment Actions

<u>Information to be addressed includes but is not limited to the following:</u> The Investigator should focus on the factors that led to the employment action that specifically relate to the Complainant. The nexus should be addressed in this paragraph; the Investigator will need to address the non-discriminatory reason the employment action occurred and specifically if that decision was based on the protected class.

Example: Dr. Laphroaig states that the Complainant was excluded from meetings because the findings of the internal investigation discovered that Complainant could not be trusted with top-secret information. Dr. Laphroaig states that the Complainant's prior EEO complaint had nothing to do with why duties were removed, nor the reason the Complainant was prohibited from confidential meetings. Dr. Laphroaig states that Dr. Octomore took over the Complainant's duties while the investigation was ongoing, and further states Dr.

Octomore was not under investigation and was cleared to work on classified projects.

Note: The point of the summary is to address relevant details and facts relevant to non-discriminatory reasons for the actions taken, not a play-by-play scenario of every statement on the affidavit.

Key tip: If the Investigator does not address relevant/ vital information, it appears as if the Investigator did not make the necessary inquiry. If Investigators are unable to obtain or extract certain information, they should draft an Investigator's Note explaining what is missing and document their attempts to obtain the information.

Complainant Witness Summary Section

- In general, the Investigator should summarize all testimony relevant to the accepted issue whether it does or does not corroborate with the Complainant's testimony.

First paragraph: Laying the Foundation

Information to be addressed includes, but is not limited to the following: The Investigator must explain the witness's position within the Agency/Division/Unit where the complaint was filed. This individual may be able to address information about the Agency's internal policies.

Example: Dr. Bowmore states that Dr. Octomore took over the duties as Lead Scientist in December of 2011. He states that Dr. Octomore now conducts all confidential experiments and relays findings during the weekly meetings.

> **Note:** Lay down the events that will lead up to why the person could/would be a viable witness. Investigators should never force a witness's testimony to corroborate with the Complainant's or anyone else's. It is common to hear different versions of the story; if something is unclear, ask follow-up questions.

Second paragraph: Addressing Context and Physical Position of Alleged Witness

<u>Information to be addressed includes but is not limited to the following:</u> It is important to illustrate how the witness was privy to information pertaining to the accepted issue. Most of the time witnesses provide circumstantial evidence rather than direct evidence, so it is effective if the Investigator writes the summary in a way to capture the context of any situation that may be considered as circumstantial evidence. For direct evidence, the Investigator must disclose position and/or note a specific source of information to potentially corroborate statements or policies.

Example: (Circumstantial Evidence): Dr. Bowmore states that all employees have been warned by Dr. Laphroaig on numerous occasions to stop questioning the purpose of laboratory assignments or else their duties and privileges would be removed.

Example: (Direct Evidence): Dr. Bowmore states that he overheard Dr. Ardbeg and Dr. Laphroaig talking in the hallway next to his office about making Complainant "the cleanup person" after he filed his EEO complaint against them. He alleges that Dr. Ardbeg told Dr.

Laphroaig, "Give Dr. Octomore his duties, that will teach him to keep his big mouth shut. He is trying to bite the hand that feeds him."

> **Note:** If something is unclear, Investigators should ask follow-up questions to distinguish exactly what that witness is referring to and the context of that situation. The "circumstantial evidence" above requires follow-up questions from the Investigator, or they will not have effectively summarized testimony from the affidavit.

Third paragraph: Nexus/Closing Statements

Information to be addressed includes but is not limited to the following: If there is a nexus, Investigators should get to the point. A witness is only a piece of the puzzle; their summary will not cover every aspect of what is generally required for sufficient fact-finding. Investigators should summarize what they have "witnessed" and move on to the next part.

***Example*:** *Dr. Bowmore states that ever since Complainant went outside of the Agency with his concerns about Agency secrets, Dr. Ardbeg and Dr. Laphroaig have retaliated against him. He alleges that Complainant told him, "They hold me here, so they can torture me over and over, so that the truth does not get out."*

> **Note:** If Complainant provides a list of 10 witnesses that have no relevant information regarding the accepted issues, Investigators should ask what information the proposed witnesses can provide before attempting to interview them. Investigators should not summarize witness information that is not relevant.

Agency Witness Section

- In general, the Investigator needs to summarize testimony relevant to the accepted issue whether it does or does not corroborate the Agency's defense.
- The Agency will usually provide a professional witness pertaining to a directive, discipline, and/or any Agency policy. These witnesses should clarify the applicable guidelines of the relevant policy. **Possible agency witnesses include** Human Resources, Employee Labor Relations, Reasonable Accommodation Coordinators, or Supervisors higher in the chain of command.

First paragraph: Laying the Foundation

<u>Information to be addressed includes, but is not limited to the following:</u> The Investigator should address the witness's position within the Agency/Division/Unit where the complaint is being filed. This individual may have pertinent information about confidentiality issues, position descriptions, and agency meetings.

Example: *Ms. Cairdeas states that she is a Human Resource Specialist. She states that she does not handle matters concerning employee Position Descriptions and assigning duties. She asserts that HR advises Management on issues concerning confidentiality for all employees in their chain of command or disciplinary procedures, if necessary.*

> **Note:** Subject Matter Experts (SME) can be fundamental in corroborating Management's non-discriminatory reasons for taking certain employment actions based on Agency policy.

Second paragraph: Addressing Context and Physical Position of Witness

<u>Information to be addressed includes, but is not limited to the following</u>: It is important to illustrate how the witness was privy to information pertaining to the accepted issue. Most of the time witnesses provide circumstantial evidence rather than direct evidence, so it is effective if the Investigator writes the summary in a way to capture the context of any situation that may be considered as circumstantial evidence. For direct evidence, the Investigator must disclose the witness's position and/or note a specific source of information to potentially corroborate statements or policies.

Example: *(Policy Defense): Ms. Cairdeas states that Management can alter an employee's privilege, duties, and/or other terms and conditions of employment if they violate the confidentiality clause and pose a potential risk and/or harm to the agency's objective.*

<u>**Note:**</u> If the summary section does reveal an expert on the subject matter in question, the Investigator should interview another person who might have knowledge concerning the employment action/policy at issue. ***Example:*** *Ms. Cairdeas states that she is unaware of any confidentiality agreement for employees and asserts that each unit has its own policies in place for specific objectives. She recommends that the third-level Supervisor (Dr. Lagavulin) could respond better to this policy.*

Third paragraph: Nexus/closing Statements

Information to be addressed includes, but is not limited to the following: The Investigator should conclude the summary quickly and effectively. Either the Agency witness knows or does not know if the employment action was based on the Complainant's protected class.

Example: *(Discrimination Defense) Dr. Lagavulin states that Mr. Ardbeg and Mr. Laphroaig are required by Agency policy to exclude employees from private meetings and/or duties when they violate the confidentiality clause. Dr. Lagavulin states that the Complainant was not retaliated against but rather the Complainant violated the Agency clause when he spoke to an outside organization concerning internal Agency matters.*

> **Note:** Usually, HR witnesses or SMEs will not have a definitive answer concerning anything to do with alleged discrimination; most responses will be related directly to policy or protocol.

Comparator Section

- In general, the Investigator should summarize testimony relevant to how the witness is a comparator by identifying his/her/their protected class, placement within the Complainant's branch/unit, similar circumstances, and how he/she/they were treated differently.
- Comparators can clarify information on alleged nexus statements if the details are presented correctly.

First paragraph: Laying the Foundation

<u>Information to be addressed includes but is not limited to the following</u>: The Investigator should outline the key variables that make the affiant a viable comparator, e.g., same position titles, co-workers under the same reporting chain, or different protected classes.

Example: *Dr. Octomore (No prior EEO activity) states that he is a Scientist, GS-14, who works in the same unit as the Complainant, Field Epidemiology Laboratory Training Program Systems (FELTPS) under the supervision of Dr. Laphroaig.*

> **Note:** The Comparator section should be brief and to the point. Comparators are not usually personally involved in the accepted issue and should rarely be interviewed. Sometimes a Comparator will be identified as a Complainant witness in an effort for the Complainant to show how that person was treated differently.

Second paragraph: Adverse Action

<u>Information to be addressed includes but is not limited to the following</u>: Address the adverse action here. A comparator should have experienced the opposite employment action compared to the Complainant.

> **Note:** If the Complainant was excluded from meetings and duties, then the comparator should have been privy to those meetings and performing duties that align with his Position Description.

Example: Dr. Octomore states that he took over the Complainant's duties and confirms that he attends weekly confidential meetings. He confirmed Complainant has not been present at those meetings lately.

Third paragraph: Conclusion

Information to be addressed includes but is not limited to the following: The Investigator should summarize whether or not the affiant experienced discrimination, based on their protected class.

Example: Dr. Octomore states that Dr. Laphroaig approached him and asked that he direct the weekly meetings until further notice. He states that he has no prior EEO activity and has not experienced retaliation of any sort.

> **Note:** Summarize the Comparator's specific experience so that the reader of the ROI can compare the Complainant's experience to that of the "Comparator's" experience.

Rebuttal Section

- In general, the Investigator should summarize rebuttal testimony as it relates to pretext. Do not restate previously summarized testimony.

Example: Complainant states that the Agency is directing Dr. Ardbeg to use Agency policies to cover his employment actions. Complainant states that if Dr. Ardbeg fired him, instead of removing his duties, the unit would have no way of preventing him (Complainant) from disclosing more information. The Complainant states that the confidentiality agreement is outdated and needs to be updated to *address new laws, government procedures, and employee rights and responsibilities; therefore, it is not a sufficient document to protect privacy issues but rather a deterrent to employees and a threat to job security.*

Statistical Breakdown Instructions

When data is received from the Agency, the Investigator should present the data in a way that puts like or related employees into groups, so they can be compared.

Below is an example based on the accepted issue for Complainant:

The Agency reported that there were 10 Scientists, GS-15, in the same division and unit that Complainant worked in. Out of 10 Scientists: nine (9) or 90% had no prior EEO activity on record, and one (1) or 10% had prior EEO activity, which was the Complainant.

Out of 10 employees, eight (8) or 80% were not under investigation at the time of the incident, and two (2) or 20% were under investigation, including Complainant and Dr. Islay. Only Complainant was excluded from confidential meetings, while Dr. Islay was on unpaid suspension.

Tip: Using a percentage is another way to detail the variable being presented. This is effective in showing possible disparity which could be key supporting circumstantial evidence.

Tip: It is helpful to show to which group Complainant belongs for comparison purposes.

In addition to the sections above, Investigators will organize relevant documents into an Index or Table of Contents which will be part of the ROI. After this step, the ROI has been drafted and is complete.

The purpose of the ROI is significant, and its quality is detrimental to the EEO complaints process.

Utilization of the ROI:

Submitted to the Agency to fulfill a requirement mandated by the EEOC.
Submitted to the Complainant and Representative for review.
Submitted/Utilized for a Final Agency Decision and/or
Submitted/Utilized by the Administrative Law Judge for the record/review.

This chapter has provided a practical guide to utilizing EEO theory, testimony, and data obtained during the investigative stage. Investigators should continuously hone their skills and challenge themselves to set the bar high in a far-reaching industry that requires highly skilled and experienced professionals.

Working on Investigator Skills (Self Exercises)

This is a bonus chapter for Investigators to practice and test their skills. This is a great personal assessment to identify areas where more knowledge or training is necessary.

As mentioned in earlier chapters, the initial 32 hours of training do not adequately provide practical application to navigate the investigative stage. An Investigator's skills are actually obtained through their frequency of hands-on experience.

> **Note:** There is nothing wrong with the 32-hour requisite training, it simply does not produce the best-in-class Investigators on its own.

The experience of an Investigator is determined by the variety, complexity, and number of cases they have investigated.

This chapter is useful for both new and seasoned Investigators, as we have provided typical circumstances, as well as rare situations that many Investigators have never faced in their careers, and will address many misconceptions of the investigative stage.

Let's get started with some practical exercises.

Exercise #1: Interpreting Accepted Issues

This exercise will familiarize and strengthen an Investigator's knowledge of different types of complaints. Understanding the issue, acknowledging the correct Prima Facie, and knowing when to ask the Agency for clarification prior to commencement is imperative.

Below, read the incident and answer the questions that follow.

(1): Accepted issue: Margaret Stevie is a Black female who has applied for a position and was not selected. The person selected for the position was a white Male in his 30s.

(Q) What are the Complainant's protected classes? What is the adverse action? Is any pertinent information missing?

_____

_____

_____

_____

_____

(2): Accepted issue: Michael Landcaster is a 65-year-old male who received a "Minimally Satisfactory" review on his Performance Management Appraisal Plan (PMAP). Other employees who are 40 years old and younger received "Fully Successful" PMAPs.

(Q) What are the Complainant's protected classes? What is the adverse action? Is any pertinent information missing?

_____

_____

_____

_____

_____

(3): Accepted issue: Zapora Williams is a light-skinned African American female that was not promoted to the next GS grade. Another employee, a dark-skinned African American female received a promotion for two consecutive years.

(Q) What are the Complainant's protected classes? What is the adverse action? Is any pertinent information missing?

_____

_____

_____

_____

_____

(4): Accepted issue: In October 2013, Julia Jewitt (Complainant) (white female), found out that she will be promoted to the next GS grade. In January 2014, Complainant found out from the HR Specialist that other male employees that had been promoted to the same GS grade as she but had received a 7% increase to their salary while she only received a 3% increase.

(Q) What are the Complainant's protected classes? What is the adverse action? Is any pertinent information missing?

_____

_____

_____

_____

_____

(5): Accepted issue: Abioye "Mark" Mustaf (African, male) was charged 5.5 hours of Absence Without Leave (AWOL).

(Q) What are the Complainant's protected classes? What is the adverse action? Is any pertinent information missing?

_____

_____

_____

_____

_____

(6): Accepted issue: Susie Cole, (Disability: physical and mental) has requested that her supervisor grant her three days of Telework because she gets depressed and has panic attacks and cannot drive during these attacks. The Supervisor denied Complainant's request for telework.

(Q) What are the Complainant's protected classes? What is the adverse action? Is any pertinent information missing?

_____

_____

_____

_____

_____

Additionally, Ms. Cole's telework has been denied and she filed an EEO discrimination case against the Management officials (RMOs). After the RMOs found out that Ms. Cole (the Complainant) had initiated an EEO case of discrimination against them, they subsequently assigned her duties that she (Ms. Cole) was not qualified to perform and assignments for which she had no training.

(Q) What are the Complainant's protected classes? What is the adverse action? Is any pertinent information missing?

_____

_____

_____

_____

_____

(7): Accepted issue: Mr. Greg Wilson (disabled veteran) has requested that his immediate Supervisor grant him five days of telework but was denied. His immediate Supervisor has allowed other disabled veterans to telework for five days a week.

(Q) What are the Complainant's protected classes? What is the adverse action? What theory of discrimination is relevant for this example? Is any pertinent information missing?

_____

_____

_____

_____

(8): Accepted issue: Jacqulyn "Jac" Tran (female, Asian, weak heart) is an International Travel Sales Executive. In March 2014, the Complainant received a note from the doctor stating that due to her health, she should not be traveling long hours, and this note was included in her personnel file. The Complainant's Supervisor read the doctor's note in her personnel file and denied her promotion months later stating that she did not meet the basic requirements for a promotion.

(Q) **What are the Complainant's protected classes? What is the adverse action? Is any pertinent information missing?**

_____

_____

_____

_____

_____

(9): Accepted issue: Dr. Julian Grant (male, Caucasian) overheard his co-worker making derogatory comments about same-sex marriage, using the term "gays" and made references to the Bible. The co-worker who was making the comment was aware that Mr. Grant (the Complainant), has been married to his same-sex partner for 10 years and this is not the first time his co-worker has made these types of comments.

(Q) **What are the Complainant's protected classes? What is the adverse action? What theory of discrimination could be relevant to this example? Is any pertinent information missing?**

_____

_____

_____

(10): Accepted issue: Dr. Grant had complained to his supervisor about his co-worker, Mr. John Mahan, in regard to the derogatory comments. Management had requested that Mr. Klein attend LBGT training and sexual discrimination training. Mr. Mahan (male, Catholic) has raised a harassment complaint against the Management officials for allegedly forcing him to attend meetings that are against his religious beliefs.

(Q) What are the Complainant's protected classes? What is the adverse action? Is any pertinent information missing?

_____

_____

_____

_____

_____

(11): Accepted issue: Ms. Natalie Washington (Female, late 20s, Spain) was hired for an assistant position within the Agency. Mr. Butler (male, late 40s, France), the Complainant's direct Supervisor, always comments on the Complainant's shoes, sends her flowers anonymously, and brings her chocolate-shaped hearts. When the Complainant refuses

Mr. Butler's advances he subsequently assigns her to do other employees' work in addition to her assigned duties and threatens her with disciplinary actions and termination of her employment.

(Q) **What are the Complainant's protected classes? What is the adverse action? What is the theory of discrimination? Is any pertinent information missing?**

_____

_____

_____

_____

_____

(12): Accepted issue: Nate "Dagen" Jamieson (Rastafarian) was not offered to work overtime hours in the employee kitchen because protocols in the kitchen prohibited facial hair and head wraps when working around food.

(Q) **What are the Complainant's protected classes? What is the adverse action? What is the theory of discrimination? Is any pertinent information missing?**

_____

_____

_____

Exercise #2: Drafting Questions

This exercise offers practical experience and training to become a seasoned Investigator. Drafting questions helps with strategizing an effective purview of the accepted claims, which eliminates irrelevant questions and hones the Investigator's skills in being thorough and concise.

Below, read the incident and draft proposed questions for the Complainant and RMOs.

Jack Frost (Complainant)

Accepted Issue: Jack Frost, Mechanical Technician, states that he was discriminated against based on race (Caucasian), on July 1, 2020, when he was denied the opportunity to attend Bookkeeping training by his Supervisor, Suzanne Summer.

Accepted Issue: Jack Frost states that he was harassed and subjected to a hostile work environment based on his sex (Male), on July 2, 2020, and continuing when his Supervisor, Suzanne Summer (Female) refused to listen to his ideas, talks in a loud voice to him, and humiliates him in front of staff in the following ways:

a. She calls him "little man" when she is looking for him. Ms. Summer says:
b. "You walk through the cubicles like a runway model."
c. "I'm jealous of your hairless legs; you go girl!"
d. "You're the reason why a woman would rather be lonely and have a cat."

e. "Jack, you're running out of options, neither woman nor men are attracted to you."

f. "You, Eric, and Dominic are pigs with suits. Do not comment on my figure again.;" and

g. "Are you going bald? Never mind, it is not like you have a choice."

Accepted Issue: Jack Frost claims discrimination based on his disability (Multiple Personality Disorder) when he was denied Reasonable Accommodation on July 3, 2020, by his Supervisor Suzanne Summer.

Accepted Issue: Jack Frost claims retaliation based on prior EEO activity and age (41), when Ms. Suzanne Summer called him a "PITA" ("Pain in the Ass") and assigned him undesirable duties on July 4, 2020.

Accepted Issue: Jack Frost claims discrimination based on short stature when he was not selected for the Supervisor Mechanical Technician position, on July 5, 2020.

Accepted Issue: On July 6, 2020, Jack Frost claims discrimination based on his religion (Flat Earther), national origin (Human), sex (LGBT), race (Caucasian), and prior EEO activity (multiple cases) when he did not follow directives from his supervisor, which resulted in him being constructively discharged.

Exercise #3: Communication

Investigators are a valuable source of information during the investigative stage.

This exercise forces an Investigator to pay attention to detail, contemplate which words they use, decide the best way to present information, and encourages them to research for specific facts.

Below, read the incident and determine if the statement is factually correct or not. If not correct, change the wording so the communication is clear, effective, and truthful.

Factual or Not:

(1) I am a neutral fact finder, and my job is to investigate your case, collect evidence, and determine if discrimination occurred.

Factual _____ **Not Factual** _____

(2) You have 180 days until your investigation expires unless you file for an amendment with the EEOC. Check their website at www.eeoc.gov.

Factual _____ **Not Factual** _____

(3) I think your case is unique, but I do not make any determinations of merit during or after the investigative stage.

Factual _____ **Not Factual** _____

(4) A Complainant has the right to extend the investigative period. How much time do you need?

Factual _____ **Not Factual** _____

(5) After the Investigative stage, I will provide you with Management's statements for rebuttal purposes.

Factual _____ **Not Factual** _____

(6) Your testimony will not be anonymous unless you sign a form that protects your confidentiality during the formal complaint stage.

Factual _____ **Not Factual** _____

(7) After receiving your Report of Investigation from the Agency, you will have the option of choosing a Final Agency Decision or a hearing in front of an Administrative Law Judge.

Factual _____ **Not Factual** _____

(8) The Complainant has the right to representation during the formal complaint process.

Factual _____ **Not Factual** _____

(9) The Complainant's representative does not have to be a lawyer.

Factual _____ **Not Factual** _____

(10) I will interview a few character witnesses to make sure the Complainant is trustworthy.

Factual _____ Not Factual _____

(11) The Investigator must listen to the Complainant's desires and try their best to meet their needs within the statutory timeframes.

Factual _____ Not Factual _____

(12) The Complainant has 15 days to provide their affidavit or respond to written interrogatories, if they do not meet the deadline, the Investigator can move forward with the complaint.

Factual _____ Not Factual _____

(13) You must interview everyone who was privy to Complainant's accepted issues.

Factual _____ Not Factual _____

(14) If a Complainant has a Representative that is an attorney, contact the Representative first. If the Representative does not respond, then copy the Complainant.

Factual _____ Not Factual _____

(15) The Complainant is the customer; it is their case. Therefore, you must accommodate them during the investigative process.

Factual _____ Not Factual _____

(16) The Investigator's neutral role is no longer necessary when Agency-provided documents reveal the Complainant was at fault and lied during testimony. You are to notify the POC immediately.

Factual _____ **Not Factual** _____

(17) The Complainant has the right to appeal their complaint to a higher level if the Investigator forgets to interview a key witness.

Factual _____ **Not Factual** _____

EEO Investigators should challenge themselves to consistently improve their skills and set the bar high. That is why we are providing advanced EEO solutions for those who desire success and want to be effective in this industry.

No one is going to force the Investigator to do more than average, basic, standard, acceptable work or "the bare minimum." Given the minimum training requirements, the onus is on the individual to get the necessary experience to be considered a highly qualified professional in the industry.

There are EEO Professionals who have prepared themselves for success, which is what we will discuss in the next and closing chapter of this book. We will address some of their secrets to producing an effective ROI.

CHAPTER 11

Five Pillars to Quality EEO Investigations

There is a popular phrase commonly made to aspiring professionals "Look to your left and look to your right. In three years only one of you will remain." This statement is true for EEO Investigators.

There are often personal reasons why aspiring Investigators do not make the cut. However, the purpose of this guide is to demonstrate how to conduct effective investigations, so the focus will be on why some EEO Investigators are successful and how they learned to conduct quality EEO Investigations.

Once Investigators decide to act by constantly learning new things, having a purpose, and working on their practical and interpersonal skills, they are preparing themselves to execute effectively in this industry.

Purpose

What motivates an individual to be involved in this industry, strive to be an effective EEO Investigator, and provide a quality ROI? When interviewing a consultant for an opportunity, AES wants to understand why the individual chose this industry. Will they be working full-time or part-time? What truly motivates this person? Is it to make a difference, a change in career choice, or for supplemental income? Finding out the person's "why" allows us to gauge their dedication and determine if they have the perseverance necessary to be a qualified professional. Having a strong purpose will provide the fuel needed to endure the learning curve on the journey to becoming successful in this industry.

Learning Curve

What is the learning curve? It is the rate of a person's progress in learning all the practical skills, techniques, and strategies required to be an Investigator. Training cannot prepare a person for the learning curve because each situation, problem, and requirement is unique. Gaining knowledge and confidence from hands-on experience and acquiring the ability to learn and think on your feet is priceless wisdom only gained while being tested during the initial learning stages. After an Investigator has investigated multiple cases, examined different theories of discrimination, learned about multiple employment incidents, and dealt with different personalities, a level of comfort sets in. Once the consultant has enough personal experience, and has experienced and overcome obstacles, they can easily assess situations and implement actions that have proven results.

Continuous Training

Whether an Investigator is inexperienced, seasoned, incompetent, or the "best in class," everyone needs continuous training. To be among the best in the field, Investigators must continuously challenge themselves. The onus is on the individual to confirm their weaknesses, develop certain skill sets, and find effective ways to streamline their services. The yearly eight-hour training requirement is structured to introduce new industry laws but is not customized to enhance an individual's skill set. Investigators who are willing to take constructive feedback, implement new skills, and commit to improving themselves through continuous training are the ones best suited for EEO Investigations long-term.

Skills

Many years ago, before social media, it was difficult to find opportunities to conduct EEO Investigations and the industry was almost a secret. If you knew the right person, you could "walk in the door" with a 32-hour certificate and start investigating employment discrimination cases. Fast forward to today, and there are now many resources to help someone become a "Certified Investigator" and there are a large variety of Vendors advertising opportunities for training.

With the current online exposure, there is a lot of competition with other newly certified investigators who are vying for the same opportunities. One of our industry peers always says that a hopeful Investigator has to "find a way to stand out from the crowd." The industry is always looking for **Qualified Investigators**, not just individuals with a certificate looking for an opportunity.

After reading this book, EEO Investigators now have a blueprint for success. The practical instructions and skills noted in this book will transform an applicant with a certificate that reads "Certified Investigator" into a valued EEO Investigator.

At Advanced EEO Solutions, we receive many inquiries from EEO Investigators looking for opportunities. First, we present applicants with a **skills test**. Then we give a free assessment of their work and only provide opportunities to the qualified Investigators.

If being a qualified Investigator is a goal, implementing instructions from this book will change your life immediately. This is an informational guide that uncovers and solves problems and prepares an Investigator to produce quality EEO Investigations.

The Qualified EEO Investigator

The qualified Investigator is a dedicated professional, not a unicorn. They are naturally hardworking, committed to the craft, and strive to give their best on every case file. They are naturally inquisitive and resourceful.

Everyone in the industry reaps the benefits of working with a qualified Investigator. The Agency desires quality ROIs: therefore, qualified Investigators are in high demand, sought after, and often requested for cases.

Conversely, if an Investigator does not invest in skill training and is not dedicated to providing a quality work product, they could eventually be on the "no use list" with Vendors or banned by certain Agencies.

AES has detailed the soft and interpersonal skills that complement the EEO knowledge and practical skills necessary to be successful. Unfortunately, we have seen talented Investigators be denied future opportunities because of their lack of people skills, overwhelming aggressiveness, lack of patience, curt responses, and other unprofessional actions. Agencies want the best, and word of an Investigator's poor behavior often spreads fast.

Reading this book is the next step towards being a successful EEO Investigator which results in quality EEO Investigations, comprehensive ROIs, and an effective EEO complaints process.

Testimonials:

I was fortunate to work alongside Garrison Birckett, AES President, and his team for several years. Through our collaboration, I progressed from Senior Investigator to Case Manager for one of the largest federal agencies in the United States. AES was an essential partner in my professional development, providing guidance and support as I navigated the complexities of the job. Their dedication to quality and passion for success instilled in me the skills necessary to become a Program Manager and Director of EEO, overseeing multiple federal contracts. Even today, I still rely on the valuable insights AES shared with me. I am grateful for the significant impact AES has made on my career and the organizations they have worked with. It was a privilege to learn from them, and I look forward to the opportunity to continue our collaborative work in the future.

Tanya S-O

I, James Hess, started my career as an EEO Investigator in June 2008 after retiring from federal service. My government career was as an Operations Manager with the United States Postal Service. During my career, I had no experience with Human Resources or Equal Employment Opportunity other than through my direct reports, which made getting started in EEO investigations a difficult task to say the least. I started working with vendors I found on the EEO contractor site, many different vendors. However, I received little or no training and assistance during the start of my second career. It was hard for me to learn on the go and receive the guidance necessary to make me a good EEO investigator.

When I started working with Mr. Birckett in or around 2012 my EEO career started to become much more fulfilling. I finally received the type of training necessary to become a good EEO investigator and provide a quality work product. Since 2012 and through today working with AES I still am not perfect by any means but have received comments and corrections on my submitted Investigative Plans, Document Requests, and Reports of Investigation that have helped me immensely. Over the years I have kept on file most of the past comments and corrections and continuously open and review based on the type of new case I receive and use as a format for success and guidance. I now have close to a complete file of different types of cases I use with all the comments and corrections I review to try not to make the same mistakes again. Over the last few years, I have learned from AES not to hurry through investigations but to take my time and continuously review my work. One mistake I made in the past was to wait and start my ROI after I received all the documents and affidavits, which was wrong. Now, I start a draft ROI after the IP/DR are approved and open and begin ROI summary as I receive returned affidavits and documents, etc., this has helped me a lot.

AES has provided me with the support and assistance I needed trying to get started in something that was a new tool for me. I have always been a supporter of the term, "Continuous Improvement," and AES has allowed me to work through mistakes and issues, make corrections, learn from them, and move to the next investigation. This has made me a better investigator and I appreciate the support I have received and hope I can continue doing EEO investigations for many years to come.

James Hess

I am a new EEO Investigator, I obtained my EEO Investigator Certification in January 2023. I sent 40-50 emails to EEO Agencies nationwide but no one was willing to work with a brand new investigator. In March 2023 I received a reply from AES and Garrison was willing to give me a chance and guide me through my first cases. AES was the only agency willing to mentor me and assist me as I started my career as an EEO Investigator.

AES has a high standard of quality work but they are there to guide you through every step of the way. AES is always willing and available to assist with questions, whether it be procedural or handling complex case issues. The agency encourages investigators' professional growth and learning.

AES is the reason I have an EEO career and I am truly grateful because this is a life-changing career change that gives me financial freedom as well as work-life balance.

S. Davis, EEO Investigator

"Garrison Birckett and Advanced EEO Solutions, LLC are outstanding leaders in EEO Investigations. Have worked for other EEO contractors but have found Garrison to be the most professional and thorough in his knowledge and guidance. Truly a pleasure to work with and learn from his experience in EEO investigations."

Ron Bell, EEO Investigator

"I have been investigating since March 2016 and began working with AES early in my career. Working with AES has been one of my best career decisions. Garrison Birckett continues to share his extensive knowledge of EEO investigations with me, and his mentorship has helped me become the successful investigator I am today. Garrison has always been available to listen and help me overcome investigation issues and streamline my caseload. I have gained a wealth of knowledge, skills, and experience working with AES, and I am very grateful to have the opportunity to continue being part of such a great EEO team."

Denise Goldner

The testimonials above reflect action and success by following the practices that we have illustrated in the book.

CONCLUSION

A Call to Action

Taking action in this industry means an EEO Investigator making the commitment, taking the steps, and implementing the tools necessary to move towards being the best in class while investigating claims of discrimination.

Why taking action is important

Reading this book is the first step towards producing quality EEO Investigations. It provides value through examples, practical instruction, and proven techniques. One of the most overlooked steps in the Investigator's progress is provided in **Chapter 10**, Self-Assessment.

When it comes to EEO Investigations, you need to combine knowledge and practical skills through repetition. When I trained EEO Investigators during the 32-hour certification class, I told them, "It's best to practice with me, make errors, ask questions, get nervous, and adjust because when a real case starts you need to be polished."

Many of the successful Investigators we have spoken with have mentioned, "We wish we would have started earlier." Why wait?

The blueprint has been provided and a path has been paved. Anyone can be a qualified EEO Investigator who is effective at conducting EEO Investigations and can properly produce a high-quality ROI.

Purpose for taking action

This is a career that affects us all, or someone close to us. Qualified EEO professionals have a rewarding occupation and can make an impact by taking a professional role in investigating discrimination in the workplace.

For every professional that takes action to improve, it will make a difference in other people's lives both directly and indirectly. AES acted, and our dreams are now a reality. We went into business with the purpose of assisting EEO professionals, and now we can do that on a larger scale with this book.

Everyone involved in the complaints process has a responsibility.

We have worked with many EEO Professionals (Investigators, EEO Specialists, Managers, and Directors) who have set the bar high. Unfortunately, there are some individuals that are dangerous to the complaints process. Without regulation of training criteria, the industry has a situation where not every Complainant has an equal or suitable experience in the complaints process. Complainants may receive a subpar experience based on who is assigned to their case.

The industry cannot afford for the EEO complaints process to be compromised any further. We need true professionals who are highly skilled and motivated.

Here are the common industry excuses used by Investigators to impede their own advancement: "This is how I have always done it," "I am already a certified Investigator," "I have been Investigating cases since the 80s," "That is not what the other company told me to do," "No one ever said something was wrong before," "Is there a short cut to save time?" "I don't need assistance, I've done X cases," "I don't have time for that," "They don't pay enough for that kind of detail," "Who is going to care?," and "They don't have a case, it's not necessary to get that information."

Do not be one of these people. Now is the time to take the steps that will result in positive change for your own career and for the industry at large.

The result of action

The industry needs best-in-class professionals to handle discrimination cases - professionals who can make a difference in the fight against discrimination in the workplace.

Qualified EEO professionals work so the individuals in the examples below have an equal opportunity in the workplace environment.

Picture the worker who was recently fired because their manager retaliated against them. They have a family to support, young kids, and a mortgage payment to make.

Imagine the disabled employee who needs ramp access so they can reach their workstation without the possibility of injuring themselves.

Then there is Ms. Washington who obtained a degree from a prestigious college like her colleagues and has been promoted after years of hard work, only to find out that she is paid 20% less than the males in the same position, with the same exact duties.

How about the 65-year-old man, who applies to countless job openings only to find out the positions were given to much younger applicants with less experience?

There are employees who wake up, get ready and dressed for the day, and fight traffic like other commuters, but when they arrive at the office, they are treated differently based on their skin color.

There is Larry who was on the fast track to climb the corporate ladder and highly regarded by Management, until he found out that his supervisor no longer considers him for promotions after learning that he was in a same-sex marriage.

Then there is Jed, who was wrongfully accused of sexual harassment and put on administrative leave after Terri made up lies about him making sexual comments; the internal investigation discovered that all co-workers testified it was Terri who was making sexual comments to Jed which made him visibly uncomfortable.

Do these examples resonate with you? Do you feel the issues are noteworthy and need to be addressed by the highest quality professionals?

To be able to work on these cases is a privilege. Investigating discrimination complaints is a prestigious profession. The above scenarios are significant, and they resonate with those destined for this industry.

Having the necessary knowledge and skills allows professionals to execute their part in the complaints process that was created to fight workplace discrimination.

Consequences of not taking action

Simply knowing and understanding EEO law is not enough to produce effective EEO Investigations. There are multiple skill sets that need to be honed, and, of course, some common sense goes a long way.

Below are real examples.

Example #1: One Investigator kept receiving complaints about his communication skills that came across as being too direct. He was truly knowledgeable in EEO and produced a great ROI. However, he was banned from the Agency for failing to address his poor interpersonal skills. **(Reference Chapter 4)**

Example #2: Many Investigators are nervous to take on larger cases, due to the extra work required. As a result, they miss many opportunities to practice, learn, and master new skill sets which are obtained through hands-on experience. **(Reference Chapter 1)**

Example #3: There was an Investigator who had one case, but he wanted to take on multiple cases, before finishing his first one. He was advised to get through a few cases before trying to handle multiple cases at a time. However, he took multiple cases from different Vendors and did not have the experience or knowledge of how to expedite testimony and documents when deadlines approached. The cases bottlenecked, deadlines were missed, and he lost future opportunities along with his reputation being damaged. **(Reference Chapter 3)**

Example #4: We once had an Investigator who always turned down non-selection cases or made excuses for not taking them. After missing valuable experience, one of their active cases was amended with a non-selection claim and they struggled and embarrassed themselves after being considered a seasoned Investigator. **(Reference Chapter 10)**

Example #5: Too many new EEO Investigators wanted to take multiple cases too early, and it usually did not end well. They either provided mediocre quality, got burnt out, or missed deadlines. **(Reference Chapter 1)**

It is no longer a secret that one of the major problems in the industry is insufficient training requirements. It is only a matter of time before compliance practices are implemented, and only those with adequate knowledge, skills, and the drive for continuous improvement will be prepared and chosen for EEO Investigations.

Professionals should learn and execute their role at a high level; the industry does not expect any one person to be the solution, but rather to be a part of the solution.

This book was meant to motivate Investigators to improve. After reading this book, each EEO professional now has detailed examples of how to be successful. AES is hoping to plant a seed and provide the first drop of water in the growth cycle.

Please take this first step to improve. Not only people in the industry, but employees nationwide rely on us to be highly qualified professionals.

If you are committed to making a difference, please reach out to us at info@advancedeeosolutions.com.

WORD GLOSSARY

AES: Advanced EEO Solutions, LLC

EEO: Equal Employment Opportunity

POC: Point of Contact

ROI: Report of Investigation

TOC: Table of Contents

CP: Complainant

RMO: Responding Management Official or Responsible Management Official

AJ: Administrative Law Judge

IC: Independent Contractor

Vendor: Government contractor that hires EEO Investigators

LOA: Letter of Acceptance or Letter of Authorization

IP: Investigative Plan

DR: Document Request

QUID: Qualified Individual with a Disability

HWE: Hostile Work Environment

MTF: Memorandum to the File

PF: Prima Facie

SF-50/52: Notification of Personnel Action/Request for Personnel Action

SOW: Statement of Work

PWS: Performance Work Statement